Approval

I0434980

Approved by: _____

Robert A. Mocny   Date
Director, US-VISIT

Record of Changes

No.	Date	Reference: Page, Table, Figure, Paragraph	A = Add. M = Mod. D = Del.	Change Description
1	3-2-2010	Entire document	M	Edited and reformatted.

Executive Summary

This document was developed by the Information Sharing and Technical Assistance Branch of the United States Visitor and Immigrant Status Indicator Technology (US-VISIT) Program as a primary reference for implementing biometric standards requirements for US-VISIT systems. It provides a baseline for implementing new and improved biometric technologies, capabilities, and services, with the aim of promoting and achieving maximum stakeholder interoperability. The information in this document will support the development of US-VISIT data-sharing agreements with other U.S. Government agencies and foreign government partners.

This document –

- Identifies biometric-related standards and implementation options to which US-VISIT currently conforms
- Provides information on current U.S. and international standards and options that US-VISIT will implement by FY 2011 to support new biometric technologies and services and to enhance interoperability with its Federal partners and other stakeholders

This version of the document focuses on specification of standards for –

- Biometric data format standards for the collection, storage, and exchange of fingerprints and palm prints, two-dimensional face images, and iris images
- Biometric transmission profiles required for data sharing with US-VISIT partners and stakeholders

The document will be updated and expanded as needed to –

- Reflect the revision or development of new standards affecting US-VISIT systems operations
- Support interoperability schemes and data-sharing agreements as they are developed among US-VISIT, its partners, and stakeholders
- Support the planning for and implementation of new technologies adopted by US-VISIT and Department of Homeland Security (DHS) components
- Support conformance and performance testing of US-VISIT biometric systems

US-VISIT systems provide identity verification and analysis services and data-sharing capabilities to multiple stakeholders, including the Departments of Justice, Defense, and State; DHS components; the Intelligence Community; State and local law enforcement agencies; and a growing list of foreign government partners. To serve this diverse mix of stakeholders, US-VISIT systems currently accommodate several formats and methods for data exchange.

US-VISIT is expanding its biometric systems capabilities to meet new requirements for biometric services among a diverse customer base. The US-VISIT Biometric Needs Assessment[1] identified a need for US-VISIT systems to accommodate the storage, extraction, and matching of new modalities, such as face and iris, and to integrate biographic and biometric data more

---

[1] Biometric Needs Assessment, US-VISIT, August 3, 2009.

effectively. In addition, US-VISIT must meet the mission objectives of National Security Presidential Directive 59 (NSPD-59)/Homeland Security Presidential Directive 24 (HSPD-24) entitled, "Biometrics for Identification and Screening to Enhance National Security." In essence, this requires US-VISIT to coordinate the sharing of biometric and associated biographic and contextual information with other Federal agencies and foreign partners in accordance with applicable law, including international obligations undertaken by the United States.[2]

US-VISIT participates in the development of new standards as required to influence the publication and adoption of standards that are of interest to US-VISIT and its stakeholders. Standards development organizations (SDOs), such as the InterNational Committee for Information Technology Standards (INCITS) M1 and the International Standards Organization Joint Technical Committee 1 (JTC 1)/Subcommittee (SC 37, Biometrics), are revising and developing new standards to support additional biometric modalities and other advances in biometric technology, including biometric sample quality, conformance, and performance testing. In addition, American National Standards Institute/National Institute of Standards and Technology (ANSI/NIST)-based biometric standards, which are widely used by the law enforcement community, are being revised to support the use of extensible markup language (XML), with the intent of replacing the older method of defining data via the use of tagged fields.

The Registry of USG Recommended Biometric Standards (August 2009)[3] makes recommendations "…based upon interagency consensus on biometric standards required to enable the interoperability of various Federal biometric applications, and guides Federal agencies as they develop and implement biometric programs." US-VISIT supports the development of standards for the registry and implements standards consistent with the registry. Acccordingly, US-VISIT conforms to ANSI/NIST-ITL 1-2007 and will migrate to the ANSI/NIST-ITL 2-2008 standard. The ANSI/NIST-ITL family of standards is widely used internationally. ANSI/NIST-ITL 2-2008 is XML-based and conforms to the National Information Exchange Model (NIEM).[4]

US-VISIT will continue to implement biometric standards consistent with the recommendations of the Registry of USG Recommended Biometric Standards and to encourage its stakeholders to follow suit. US-VISIT will also continue to take an active part in SDO activities to ensure that the standards development process fully considers DHS operational and technical needs.

---

[2] http://www.fas.org/irp/offdocs/nspd/nspd-59 html

[3] http://www.biometrics.gov/Standards/default.aspx

[4] NIEM provides structure, standards, and methods for defining and sharing information exchanges between and within agencies and domains, and uses XML as its rendering language. See http://www.niem.gov/index.php.

Contents

Figures

Tables

I.   Introduction

Since its inception, the United States Visitor and Immigrant Status Indicator Technology (US-VISIT) Program has provided biometric screening for Department of Homeland Security (DHS) components and has partnered with other Federal agencies in the use of biometric data for national security initiatives. The Automated Biometric Identification System (IDENT), US-VISIT's biometric database, contains fingerprint records for over 108 million subjects. IDENT is currently interoperable with the Federal Bureau of Investigation's (FBI) Integrated Automated Fingerprint Identification System (IAFIS),[5] which provides access to the biometric-based criminal history records of more than 50 million subjects. Limited data sharing with other agencies and foreign governments has also been achieved using ad hoc file transfers and manual entry processes.

To facilitate the data sharing that is at the core of what US-VISIT does, this document provides the technical standards US-VISIT uses—or will use in the near future—to implement the actual collection, storage, and transmission of biometric and associated biographic data. Use of these standards will make US-VISIT data sharing more accurate, repeatable, and reliable, which will in turn provide homeland security decisionmakers with critical identity verification data in a timely manner.

I.1   Background

US-VISIT's primary focus has been to provide fingerprint-based identity verification and analysis services to its stakeholders. US-VISIT is expanding system capabilities to meet new requirements for biometric services for its diverse customer base, which includes several DHS components, other Federal agencies, State and local agencies, and foreign governments. The US-VISIT Biometric Needs Assessment[6] identified additional needs for US-VISIT systems to accommodate the storage, extraction, and matching of iris, facial, and various formats of fingerprint biometric data, and to integrate biographic and biometric data more effectively. In addition, US-VISIT must meet the mission objectives of National Security Presidential Directive 59 (NSPD-59)/Homeland Security Presidential Directive 24 (HSPD-24) entitled, "Biometrics for Identification and Screening to Enhance National Security." In essence, this requires US-VISIT to coordinate the sharing of biometric and associated biographic and contextual information with other Federal agencies and foreign partners in accordance with applicable law, including international obligations undertaken by the United States.[7]

Biometric standards and transmission profiles that support data exchanges between US-VISIT systems and the systems of US-VISIT stakeholders are essential to the effective operation of

---

[5] http://www.fbi.gov/hq/cjisd/iafis htm

[6] Biometric Needs Assessment, US-VISIT, August 3, 2009.

[7] http://www.fas.org/irp/offdocs/nspd/nspd-59 html

US-VISIT biometric system services. The Registry of USG Recommended Biometric Standards, August 2009,[8] makes recommendations "…based upon interagency consensus on biometric standards required to enable the interoperability of various Federal biometric applications, and guides Federal agencies as they develop and implement biometric programs." US-VISIT supported development of the registry and strives to develop its biometric services to be consistent with the registry.

US-VISIT participates in the development of new standards as required to influence the publication and adoption of standards that are of interest to US-VISIT and its stakeholders. Standards development organizations (SDOs), such as the InterNational Committee for Information Technology Standards (INCITS) M1 and the International Standards Organization Joint Technical Committee 1 (JTC 1)/Subcommittee (SC 37, Biometrics), are revising and developing new standards to support additional biometric modalities and other advances in biometric technology, including biometric sample quality, conformance, and performance testing. In addition, American National Standards Institute/National Institute of Standards and Technology (ANSI/NIST)-based biometric standards, which are widely used by the law enforcement community, are being revised to support the use of extensible markup language (XML), with the intent of replacing the older method of defining data via the use of tagged fields.

Figure I-1 is a pictorial view of US-VISIT connectivity with its stakeholders. It shows the relationships of the applicable standards necessary to achieve interoperability. Table I-1 describes the types of standards identified in Figure I-1, including data collection formats, technical interfaces, data exchange and storage formats, and data transmission profiles. The transmission of data between US-VISIT systems and some international biometric systems may require accommodating legacy international standards as well as unique transaction requirements.

---

[8] The registry was developed by the National Science and Technology Council (NSTC) Subcommittee on Biometrics and Identity Management. The subcommittee continuously reviews the content of this document, and releases updated versions as required to assist agencies in the implementation and reinforcement process of biometric standards to meet agency-specific mission needs. The most recent version was published in August 2009. See http://www.biometrics.gov/Standards/default.aspx

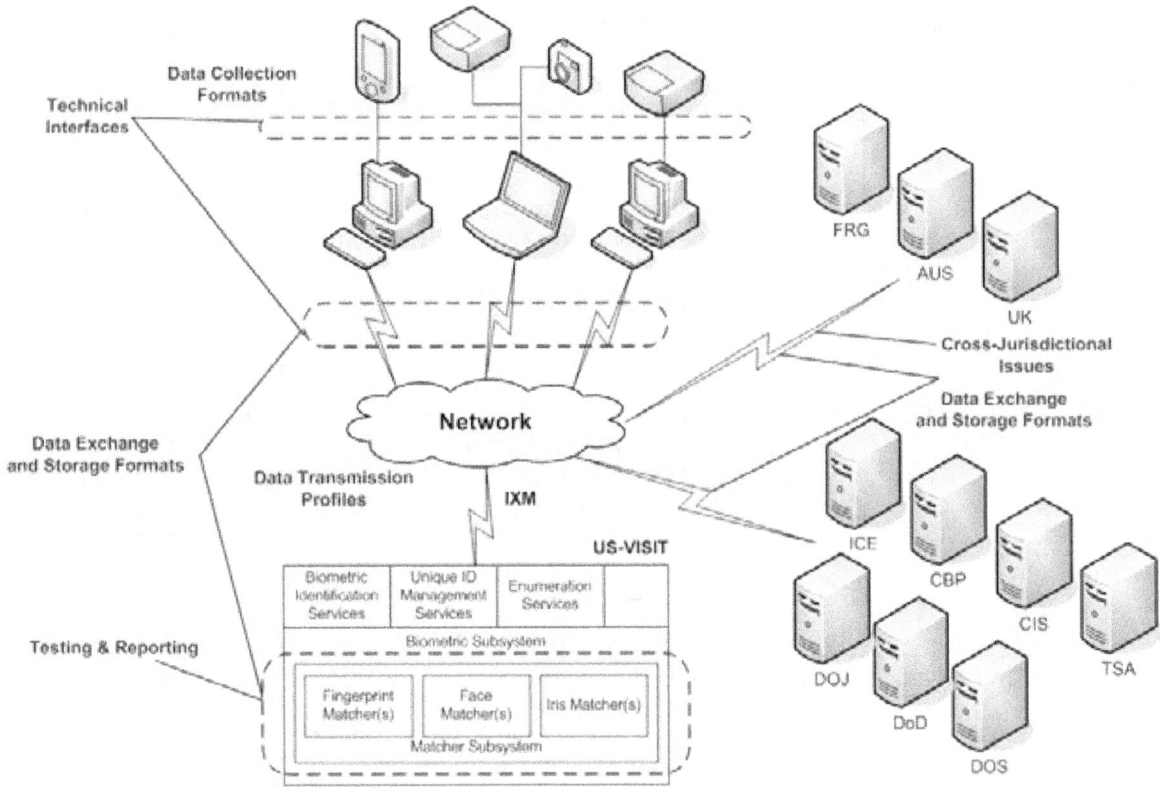

Figure I-1. US-VISIT Stakeholder Interoperability

Table I-1. Types of Biometric Standards

Type of Standard	Function	Examples[9]
Data Exchange and Storage Formats	• Specify the content, meaning, and representation of formats for the interchange of biometric data. • Specify notation and transfer formats that provide platform independence. • Separate transfer syntax from content definition.	• ANSI/NIST-ITL 1-2007 – Data Format for the Interchange of Fingerprint, Facial, and Other Biometric Information • ANSI/NIST-ITL 2-2008 Type-10 – Capture and Storage of Face Images with SAP ≥ 10 • ISO/IEC 19794-6:2005 Biometric Data Interchange Formats – Part 6: Iris Image Data
Technical Interfaces	• Specify interfaces and interactions between biometric components and subsystems. • Add plug-and-play capability to integrate system components into functioning systems and swap components as needed without losing functionality.	• ANSI INCITS 358-2002 BioAPI Specification (Version 1.1) • ANSI INCITS 398-2008 Common Biometric Exchange Formats Framework (CBEFF)
Transmission Profiles	• Facilitate interoperability. Specify application-specific criteria onto a base standard to establish definitive values for performance-related parameters in the base standard (e.g., resolution, maximum compression) or enumerating values for optional or conditional requirements (e.g., full-frontal face vs. token face).	• FBI Electronic Biometric Transmission Specification (FBI EBTS) v9.0 • DOD Electronic Biometric Transmission Specification (DOD EBTS) v2.0 • Interpol Implementation of ANSI/NIST-ITL 1-2007 (INT-I) v5.0 • IDENT Exchange Messages (IXM) Specification
Testing and Reporting	• Specify biometric performance metric definitions and calculations, approaches to test performance, and requirements for reporting the results of these tests.	• ANSI INCITS 409-2005 Biometric Performance Testing and Reporting Part 1: Principle Framework Part 2: Technology Testing Methodology Part 3: Scenario Testing Methodologies
Cross-Jurisdictional and Societal	• Address study and standardization of technical solutions to societal aspects of biometric implementations.	• ISO/IEC 24714, Cross-Jurisdictional and Societal Aspects of Implementation of Biometric Technologies • ISO/IEC 24779, Pictograms, Icons, and Symbols for Use with Biometric Systems

---

[9] See the Registry of USG Recommended Biometric Standards, Version 2.0, August 10, 2009, for additional examples.

I.2   Vision

US-VISIT is expanding its support to stakeholders by developing a future end-state vision for data exchange that will facilitate new biometric technologies and services and establish standards-based requirements for interoperability. This vision will incorporate emerging biometric standards, support additional modalities that US-VISIT expects to implement by FY 2011, and minimize the need for manual processing. The selection and adoption of standards will take into account the known or anticipated migration plans of US-VISIT stakeholders to new biometric and related data-sharing capabilities and the revision of other applicable standards expected in the next 1–2 years. US-VISIT recognizes its responsibility to stakeholders with legacy systems and will continue to support these systems until stakeholders can implement current standards.

US-VISIT will continue to implement biometric standards consistent with the recommendations of the Registry of USG Recommended Biometric Standards and will encourage its stakeholders to do the same. US-VISIT will also migrate to conformance with ANSI/NIST-ITL 2-2008, Data Format for the Interchange of Fingerprint, Facial, & Other Biometric Information – Part 2: XML Version.

In addition, US-VISIT will continue to take an active part in SDO activities to ensure that the standards development process takes into consideration DHS operational and technical needs. US-VISIT will consider and incorporate, as appropriate, those changes in standards that are consistent with its needs while maximizing interoperability with its stakeholders.

I.3   Purpose

This document was developed by the US-VISIT Information Sharing and Technical Assistance (ISTA) Branch as a reference for developing US-VISIT system-specific policy and technical documents, such as implementation plans, standard operating procedures, architecture technical views, and application profiles; and to support data-sharing agreements with other U.S. Government organizations and foreign entities. It is also intended to be a baseline for planning continued improvements to US-VISIT systems with respect to interoperability, adoption of additional biometric modalities, and new communication technologies. This document will necessarily be revised to reflect changes in the highly dynamic environment of evolving standards, adoption of new modalities and biometric quality metrics, and the ongoing migration to extensible markup language (XML) as the primary data exchange method.

This document –

- Identifies biometric-related standards and implementation options to which US-VISIT currently conforms

   Provides information on current U.S. and international standards and standards options that US-VISIT will implement by FY 2011 to support new biometric technologies and services and to enhance interoperability with its Federal partners and other stakeholders

I.4   Scope

This document –

- Describes the current status of US-VISIT's implementation of biometric-related standards and implementation options
- Identifies biometric standards and implementation options required in the next 1–2 years to support planned US-VISIT system capabilities
- Notes additional standards and options to be considered for longer term US-VISIT systems modernization

US-VISIT developed and implemented the specification for IDENT exchange messages (IXM) according to the Global Justice XML Data Model (GJXDM).[10] However, US-VISIT supports other legacy transmission profiles and standards for several of its stakeholders. The basis for automated data sharing between US-VISIT and other Federal agencies has not yet been fully defined. US-VISIT is collaborating with the Federal Bureau of Investigation (FBI) to develop full interoperability between US VISIT systems and the FBI's IAFIS, which is evolving to the Next Generation Identification (NGI)[11] system. US-VISIT and the Department of Defense (DOD) have formed an integrated project team (IPT) to develop a mutually agreeable approach for interoperability between US-VISIT systems and DOD biometric systems. As the framework for interoperability between US-VISIT and its Federal partners and among U.S. agencies and international partners is better defined, future versions of this document will provide revised and, if necessary, more detailed specifications for the standards required for automated interagency data sharing.

Standards required for information security are not addressed in this document, since security requirements for US-VISIT systems are managed by the US-VISIT Information System Security Manager. Standards or activities related to conformance and performance testing of biometric matchers, devices, and systems are currently not addressed in this document, but may be addressed in the future.

In summary, this is an evolving document that will be updated and expanded as needed to –

- Reflect the revision or development of new standards affecting US-VISIT systems operations
- Support interoperability schemes and data-sharing agreements as they are developed among US-VISIT and stakeholder agencies
- Support the planning for and implementation of new technologies adopted by US-VISIT and DHS components
- Support conformance and performance testing of US-VISIT biometric systems

---

[10] http://www.it.ojp.gov/jxdm

[11] http://www.fbi.gov/hq/cjisd/ngi htm

I.5   Document Organization

The document is organized as follows:

- Section II: Biometric Data Format Standards for Collection, Storage, and Exchange – Identifies the biometric modality-specific data representation standards and specifications that are required to achieve the end-state vision by FY 2011. This section also provides a discussion of emerging standards and required changes to existing standards.

- Section III: Biometric Transmission Profiles – Describes the methods and options for exchanging data between US-VISIT and its stakeholders, and the current status of the approaches used in US-VISIT.

- Section IV: Related Standards and Guidance – Describes additional standards and guidance that will be required to ensure biometric data quality and to support new applications.

- Section V: Standards for Future Consideration – Describes standards for new modalities and functionalities that may be used in the future.

- Section VI: Referenced Documents

- Section VII: Abbreviations and Acronyms

- Appendix A: Biometric Transaction (Service) Comparison

- Appendix B: Cross Reference by Type-2 User-Defined Field Numbers and IXM Elements

II. Biometric Data Format Standards for Collection, Storage, and Exchange

This section describes the biometric standards required for the collection, storage, and exchange of biometric data relevant to US-VISIT identification and identity analysis services. These standards address specific biometric sample formats and are the basis of the biometric transmission profiles discussed in section III. Standards shown in gray text in the tables are included for completeness and possible future consideration, but are not required by US-VISIT systems at this time. Related standards and requirements, such as standards pertaining to image quality, data compression, and mobile applications, are addressed in section IV.

To identify pertinent standards for new services and applications that are not currently addressed in this document, refer to the latest version of the Registry of USG Recommended Biometric Standards, Version 2.0, August 10, 2009.

II.1 ANSI/NIST-ITL

ANSI/NIST-ITL[12] is is the base standard for most US-VISIT biometric standards requirements. ANSI/NIST-ITL 1-2000 was the result of the merger of two documents—ANSI/NIST-CSL 1-1993, Data Format for the Interchange of Fingerprint Information, and ANSI/NIST-ITL 1a-1997, Data Format for the Interchange of Fingerprint, Facial, and SMT Information—that emphasized the tagged-field record, and introduced new record types for the exchange of recorded fingerprint, latent, and palm print images. ANSI/NIST-ITL 1-2000 was initially developed as the standardized means for the interchange of fingerprint, facial, and scars, marks, and tattoos (SMTs) within the law enforcement community. ANSI/NIST-ITL 1-2007, which revised ANSI/NIST-ITL 1-2000, defines the content, format, and units of measurement for the exchange of fingerprint, palmprint, facial/mug shot, SMT, iris, and other biometric sample information that may be used to identify or verify the identity of a subject. The information consists of a variety of mandatory and optional items, including scanning parameters, related descriptive and record data, digitized fingerprint information, and compressed or uncompressed images.

ANSI/NIST-ITL 2-2008, Part 2 XML,[13] was developed as an XML alternative for the conventional ANSI/NIST tagged-field format. A goal of part 2 is to describe a "one-to-one" correspondence of XML elements to the numerically tagged conventional elements described in part 1. The part 1 subelements (separated by the US and RS characters in the conventional representation) have been given XML counterparts in part 2.

Table II-1 briefly describes each version of ANSI/NIST-ITL and identifies the stakeholders currently using the standard.

---

[12] http://fingerprint.nist.gov/standard

[13] http://fingerprint.nist.gov/standard/xml/index.html

Table II-1. ANSI/NIST-ITL Base Standards

Name	Description	Current Modalities	Stakeholders Currently Using Standard
ANSI/NIST-ITL 1-2000	Base standard for biometric data exchange with some mandatory field requirements, optional fields, and rules for configuring options by users. Predecessor of ANSI/NIST-ITL 1-2007. Basis for FBI EFTS v7.1, DOD EBTS v1.2 and INT-I v4.22b.	Fingerprint, palmprint, face (mug shot), and SMT	Users of FBI EFTS v7.1, DOD EBTS v1.2, DOD, INT-I 4.22b (e.g., State and local law enforcement, DOD, DOJ, Interpol, Germany)
ANSI/NIST-ITL 1-2007	Base standard for biometric data exchange with some mandatory field requirements and rules for configuring options by users. Tagged field equivalent of ANSI/NIST-ITL 2-2008, Part 2 XML. Basis for FBI EBTS v8.1, DOD EBTS v2.0 and INT-I v5.0.	Fingerprint, palmprint, face, iris, other (Type-99), DNA flag field	Users of FBI EBTS v8.1 and v9.0, DOD EBTS v2.0, and INT-I v5.0 (e.g., FBI, State and local law enforcement, DOD, DOJ, Interpol).
ANSI/NIST-ITL 2-2008	XML equivalent of ANS/NIST-ITL 1-2007.	Same modalities as ANSI/NIST-ITL 1-2007	Terrorist Screening Center (TSC)

II.2   ANSI/NIST-ITL Record Types and Domain Names

ANSI/NIST ITL transactions contain one or more logical records. A logical record is "a record independent of its physical environment; portions of one logical record may be located in different physical records, or several logical records or parts of logical records may be located in one physical record."[14] (See table II-2 for a list of ANSI/NIST-ITL record types). An ANSI/NIST-ITL Type-1 logical record is mandatory and is required for each transaction. The Type-1 record provides information describing type and use or purpose for the transaction involved, a listing of each logical record included in the file, the originator or source of the physical record, the destination entity for the record, and other useful and required information items.

---

[14] ANSI/NIST-ITL 1-2007, NIST Special Publication 500-271. http://fingerprint.nist.gov/standard/

Table II-2. ANSI/NIST-ITL Logical Record Types[15]

Logical Record Type	Logical Record Content
Type-1	Transaction information
Type-2	User-defined descriptive text
Type-3	Low-resolution grayscale fingerprint image
Type-4	High-resolution grayscale fingerprint image
Type-5	Low-resolution binary fingerprint image
Type-6	High-resolution binary fingerprint image
Type-7	User-defined image
Type-8	Signature image
Type-9	Minutiae data
Type-10	Facial and SMT image
Type-11	Reserved for future use
Type-12	Reserved for future use
Type-13	Variable-resolution latent image
Type-14	Variable-resolution fingerprint image
Type-15	Variable-resolution palmprint Image
Type-16	User-defined variable-resolution testing
Type-17	Iris image
Type-18-98	Reserved for future use
Type-99	CBEFF biometric data record

Transaction codes are identifiers used in the Type-1 record to indicate the type of transaction (e.g., IDENT Exchange Message, Identify, and FBI Criminal Ten-Print Submission-Answer Required [CAR]) and the processing required for the file. Transaction codes are defined by the receiving agency (e.g., FBI, DOD, and Interpol) and reflect the varying operational needs of the stakeholders. Some of these differences are simply name differences (for example, a search and enroll request may be called something else by another stakeholder), while other differences reflect transactions that are unique to stakeholders. Appendix A compares the different transaction/service codes used to request a biometric service/search of the FBI, DOD, Interpol, or US-VISIT biometric systems.

To establish a common basis for numbering, meaning, and formatting text fields in ANSI/NIST transactions, jurisdictions that use the same general set of data fields subscribe to a common "implementation domain." An implementation domain is a group of agencies or organizations that have agreed to use specific preassigned groups of fields for exchanging information unique to their purposes. Domain names reflect the user base for each stakeholder. The FBI maintains the domain names for the law enforcement community in North America; the DOD Biometric Task Force (BTF) maintains the domain names for DOD; and Interpol maintains domain names

[15] Ibid., p. 13.

for its implementations. Checking the validity and currency of these names and mapping the domain to the correct text fields corresponding to IDENT's data model presents a challenge that must be addressed by IXM. Currently, IXM supports only the FBI's domain and has mapped FBI fields to IXM's data model; the listing of domains and mapping to IXM will need to be expanded to support data exchange with DOD's ABIS, Interpol's Automated Fingerprint Information System (AFIS), and the systems of other international groups.

While a central registry of domain names has been suggested, there is currently no active program for implementing it. Currently, the issuers of domain names maintain their own list of domain names and transaction types.

Type-2 and Type-14 are the only ANSI/NIST-ITL logical record types that have implementation differences. The following two sections discuss these differences.

II.2.1   Implementation Differences for Type-2 (Transaction, Demographic, and Biographic Information) Records

ANSI/NIST Type-2 records contain user-defined textual fields that provide identification and descriptive information associated with the subject of the transaction. Data contained in this record conforms in format and content to the specifications of the domain name found in the Type-1 record. The ANSI/NIST standards specify only the content of the first two fields in the Type-2 record. The remaining fields of the record(s) conform to the format, content, and requirements of the subscribed domain name used by the agency to which the transmission is being sent.

The Type-2 record differs somewhat for all of the transmission profiles that require processing by IDENT. There is an ongoing effort within the stakeholder community to coordinate and/or standardize the information content for interoperability purposes. IDENT recognizes the differences between the FBI EBTS and the IXM format and uses an exchange mapping scheme to address these differences. Similar mappings will likely be required for DOD, Interpol, and other international groups. The DOD EBTS uses the same field numbers as that of the FBI through field 2.096, but has added approximately 50 additional fields pertinent to its mission. Interpol has assigned different field names to many of the fields used by FBI that will require remapping to the IXM data model.

Appendix B compares differences in the Type-2 fields defined for IXM, the FBI, DOD, and Interpol, and in the current implementation agreement proposal with Germany.

II.2.2   Implementation Differences for Type-14 Records

There are several differences between the implementation of the ANSI/NIST Type-14 fingerprint image record by US-VISIT, the FBI, and DOD, and the implementation of the same record type by Interpol (INT-I). Most notably, Interpol permits maximum thumb image dimensions that may be as much as 4.6 mm (greater than for US-VISIT, FBI, and DOD). Although these differences have the potential to impact IDENT search performance, IDENT is designed to accommodate variations of this magnitude.

II.3   Modality-Specific Data Format Standards

This section describes the standards required for data exchange and the format of records for modalities that are or will be supported by US-VISIT systems.

II.3.1 Fingerprints and Palmprints

II.3.1.1 Plain and Rolled Fingerprint Images

Table II-3. Plain and Rolled Fingerprint Images

Standard	Approved Use	US-VISIT Status	Action Required
ICAO 9303	When used in addition to the ANSI/NIST-ITL, Type-4 (ISO/IEC 19794-4)	Not implemented	Assess need
ANSI/NIST-ITL 1-2000, Type-4	Capture, storage, and exchange	Implemented via IXM wrapper	Maintain support and work with stakeholders to migrate to ANSI/NIST 2-2008, Type-14[16]
ANSI/NIST-ITL 1-2007, Type-4	Capture, storage, and exchange	Not implemented	None
ANSI/NIST-ITL 1-2007, Type-14	Capture, storage, and exchange	Implemented via IXM wrapper	Maintain support
ANSI/NIST-ITL 2-2008, Type-14		Not implemented	Implement in IXM

No action is required for standards shown in gray text. These standards are included for completeness and possible future consideration.

ANSI/NIST-ITL 1-2000, Type-4 (Plain and Rolled Fingerprint Images)

Required action:

- Maintain support of the ANSI/NIST-ITL 1-2000 Type-4 record type via IXM wrapper and encourage move to ANSI/NIST-ITL 2-2008 Type-14 as soon as practical.

- Engage domestic and international stakeholders and customers in discussion about moving from Type-4 to Type-14, preferably in accordance with ANSI/NIST-ITL 2-2008.

US Registry Implementation Guidance: Capture and storage with resolution of 19.69 pixels/mm or 39.37 pixels/mm ($\pm$ 1 percent).

- When images are captured at 19.69 pixels/mm and compressed with wavelet scalar quantization (WSQ), the compression ratio shall not exceed 15:1.

- When images are captured at 39.37 pixels/mm and compressed using JPEG 2000, the compression ratio shall not exceed 15:1.

Additional Information/Guidance: While ANSI/NIST-ITL 1-2007 Type-4 remains the predominant format for the transmission of rolled fingerprint information, the Type-14 record is recommended because it is:

- Used for plain impression transactions, including segmentation coordinates.

---

[16] The current draft agreement with Germany specifies Type-4 records and the transmission profile INT-I v4.22b, which is based on ANSI/NIST-ITL 1-2000.

- Supports use of high-resolution images.
- A more flexible format for additional metadata.

ANSI/NIST-ITL 1-2007 Type-14 (Plain and Rolled Fingerprint Images [Including Identification Flats])

ANSI/NIST-ITL 2-2008 Type-14 (Plain and Rolled Fingerprint Images [Including Identification Flats]

Required Action:

- Maintain current support for ANSI/NIST-ITL 1-2007 Type-14.
- Engage domestic and international stakeholders and customers in discussion about moving from Type-4 to Type-14.
- US-VISIT should develop a plan for migration to ANSI/NIST-ITL 2-2008 Type-14 in IXM.
- Engage domestic and international stakeholders and customers in discussion about moving to ANSI/NIST-ITL 2-2008 Type-14.

US Registry Implementation Guidance: Capture and storage with resolution of 19.69 pixels/mm or 39.37 pixels/mm (± 1 percent).

- When images are captured at 19.69 pixels/mm and compressed with WSQ, the compression ratio shall not exceed 15:1.
- When images are captured at 39.37 pixels/mm and compressed using Joint Photographic Experts Group (JPEG) 2000, the compression ratio shall not exceed 15:1.

Additional Information/Guidance: None.

II.3.1.2   Latent Fingerprint and Latent Palmprint Images

The US-VISIT Biometric Support Center (BSC) currently receives latent fingerprints as ANSI/NIST-ITL Type-4 records. Latent palmprints are not currently processed by US-VISIT.

Table II-4. Latent Fingerprint and Latent Palmprint Images

Standard	Approved Use	US-VISIT Status	DHS TRM Category	Action Required
ANSI/NIST-ITL 1-2007 Type-13	Storage and exchange	Not implemented	1.4..2-A/1.4.4.3-C	Implement the ANSI/NIST-ITL 1-2007 Type-13 record type to support data exchange agreement with Germany[17]
ANSI/NIST-ITL 2-2008 Type-13	Storage and exchange	Not implemented		Implement in IXM

ANSI/NIST-ITL 1-2000 Type-13 (Latent Fingerprint and Latent Palmprint Images)

ANSI/NIST-ITL 2-2008 Type-13 (Latent Fingerprint and Latent Palmprint Images

Required Action:

- Implement the ANSI/NIST-ITL 1-2007 Type-13 record type via IXM wrapper to support the data exchange agreement with Germany. Encourage move to ANSI/NIST-ITL 2-2008 as soon as practicable.
- Develop a plan for implementing ANSI/NIST-ITL 2-2008 Type-13 in IXM.

US Registry Implementation Guidance:

- The latent image shall be acquired with a native resolution of 394 pixels/cms or greater.
- Latent images should be uncompressed. If losslessly compressed, images shall be stored in conformance to the ISO/IEC 15948 format (PNG). Images shall not be compressed using a lossy compression algorithm.
- If reduced resolution versions are prepared (e.g., for transmission), the parent high-resolution image shall be retained.

Additional Information/Guidance: None.

---

[17] The current draft agreement with Germany specifies Type-13 records and the transmission profile INT-I v4.22b, which is based on ANSI/NIST-ITL 1-2000. However, ANSI/NIST-ITL 1-2007 Type-13 records are backward compatible with ANSI/NIST-ITL 1-2000 Type-13 records.

II.3.1.3 Palmprint Images (Excluding Latent Palmprints)

Table II-5. Palmprint Images (Excluding Latent Palmprints)

Standard	Approved Use	US-VISIT Status	DHS TRM Category	Action Required
ANSI/NIST-ITL 1-2000, Type-15	Storage and exchange	Not implemented	1.4.2-A/1.4.4.3-C	Assess need to implement this record type to support data exchange agreement with Germany[18]
ANSI/NIST-ITL 1-2007, Type-15		Not implemented		None
ANSI/NIST-ITL 2-2008, Type-15		Not implemented		Implement in IXM

No action is required for standards shown in gray text. These standards are included for completeness and possible future consideration.

ANSI/NIST-ITL 1-2000 Type-15 (Palmprint Images, Excluding Latent Palmprints)

ANSI/NIST-ITL 2-2008 Type-15 (Palmprint Images, Excluding Latent Palmprints)

Required Action:

- Assess need to implement the ANSI/NIST-ITL 1-2000 Type-15 record type to support the data exchange agreement with Germany. If yes, implement ANSI/NIST-ITL 1-2000 Type-15 record type via IXM wrapper and encourage move to ANSI/NIST-ITL 2-2008 as soon as practical.
- Implement ANSI/NIST-ITL 2-2008 Type-15 in IXM.

US Registry Implementation Guidance:

- Capture and storage with resolution $\geq$ 197 pixels/cm.
- When images are captured at 197 pixels/cm and compressed with WSQ, the compression ratio shall not exceed 15:1. This may be achieved by invoking the WSQ compressor with a target bit rate parameter greater than or equal to 8/15 bits per pixel.
- When images are captured at 394 pixels/cm and compressed using JPEG 2000, the compression ratio shall not exceed 15:1. This may be achieved by invoking the JPEG 2000 compressor with a target bit rate greater than or equal to 8/10 bits per pixel.
- If images scanned at 1000 pixels per inch (ppi) and compressed using JPEG 2000 are to be converted to images at 500 ppi and compressed using WSQ, then MITRE procedures (MITRE1000) shall be followed.

Additional Information/Guidance: None.

---

[18] The current draft agreement with Germany specifies Type-15 records and the transmission profile INT-I v4.22b, which is based on ANSI/NIST-ITL 1-2000.

II.3.1.4   Fingerprint Minutiae (Excluding Latent Fingerprint Minutiae; Storage and Exchange Outside Unrelated to Personal Identity Credentials)

There are a number of standards for minutiae data exchange, many of which relate to the use of minutiae in credentialing applications. There is no established requirement for incorporating this functionality in US-VISIT systems at this time. However, this capability may be required in the future.

Table II-6. Fingerprint Minutiae (Excluding Latent Fingerprint Minutiae; Storage and Exchange Outside Unrelated to Personal Identity Credentials)

Standard	Approved Use	US-VISIT Status	DHS TRM Category	Action Required
INCITS 378-2004	Storage and exchange outside of an unrelated to personal identity credentials	Not implemented		None
ANSI/NIST-ITL 1-2007 Type-9, Fields 1-4 and 13-23				
ANSI/NIST-ITL 1-2007 Type-9, Fields 1-4 and 126-150				
ANSI/NIST-ITL 2-2008 Annex G XML encoding of INCITS 378-2004				
ANSI/NIST-ITL 2-2008 Type-9, per Table 216a and 216b				

II.3.1.5   Fingerprint Minutiae (Storage in and Transmission to Personal Identity Credentials for Match-on-Card)

US-VISIT currently has no application for this standard. However, it could have future applicability to programs such as DHS' E-Verify.

Table II-7. Fingerprint Minutiae (Storage in and Transmission to Personal Identity Credentials for Match-on-Card)

Standard	Approved Use	US-VISIT Status	DHS TRM Category	Action Required
INCITS/ISO/IEC 19794-2:2005[2008], clause 8 compact card format with clause 9 format types 0001, 0003, 0005	Storage in, and transmission to, personal identity credentials for match-on-card	Not implemented		None

No action is required for standards shown in gray text. These standards are included for completeness and possible future consideration

II.3.1.6   Fingerprint Minutiae (Storage in and Transmission to Personal Identity Credentials for Match-off-Card)

US-VISIT currently has no application for this standard. However, it could have future applicability to programs such as E-Verify.

Table II-8. Fingerprint Minutiae (Storage in and Transmission to Personal Identity Credentials for Match-off-Card)

Standard	Approved Use	US-VISIT Status	DHS TRM Status	Action Required
INCITS 378:2004	Storage in, and transmission to, personal identity credentials for match-off-card	Not implemented		None

No action is required for standards shown in gray text. These standards are included for completeness and possible future consideration

II.3.1.7   Latent Fingerprint Minutiae

The US-VISIT Biometric Support Center (BSC) is currently the only US-VISIT stakeholder that sends latent fingerprint minutiae to the US-VISIT latent processing system. A custom software and system interface developed by Cogent Computing Corporation is used to process latent fingerprint minutiae. However, a standards-based approach for submitting latent fingerprint minutiae to the US-VISIT latent processing system could be achieved by implementing ANSI/NIST-ITL 2-2008 Type-9 records.

The current draft agreement with Germany specifies Type-9 records and the transmission profile INT-I v4.22b, which is based on ANSI/NIST-ITL 1-2000. The agreement also specifies ANSI/International Committee for Information Technology Standards (INCITS) 378-2004, Fingerprint Minutiae Format for Data Interchange, for minutiae placement. Since support for

Type-9 Fields 126-140 began with ANSI/NIST-ITL 1-2007,[19] a nonstandard implementation of ANSI/NIST-ITL 1-2000 Type-9 records would be required, and the Type-9 record would likely resemble that of ANSI/NIST-ITL 1-2007.

Table II-9. Latent Fingerprint Minutiae

Standard	Approved Use	US-VISIT Status	DHS TRM Category	Action Required
ANSI/NIST-ITL 1-2007 Type-9, Fields 1-4 and 126-140	Storage and exchange	Not implemented		Implement the ANSI/NIST-ITL 1-2007 Type-9, Fields 1-4 and 126-140 record to support data exchange with Germany
ANSI/NIST-ITL 2-2008 Type-9, Tables 216a and 216b	Storage and exchange	Not implemented		Develop a plan to implement this record type in IXM

ANSI/NIST-ITL 1-2000 Type 9, Fields 1-4 and 126-150 (Latent Fingerprint Minutiae)

ANSI/NIST-ITL 2-2008 Type 9, Tables 216a and 216b (Latent Fingerprint Minutiae)

Required Action:

- Implement ANSI/NIST-ITL 2-2007 Type-9, Fields 1-4 and 126-140, record via IXM wrapper to support the data exchange agreement with Germany and encourage move to ANSI/NIST-ITL 2-2008 as soon as practical.

- Develop a plan to implement ANSI/NIST-ITL 2-2008, Type-9, Tables 216a and 216b, in IXM with support of the pertinent IDENT vendor-specific latent encoding scheme(s). This capability would support BSC submission of minutiae-based latent searches as well as potential such searches by other stakeholders.

US Registry Implementation Guidance: Standardized minutiae records afford only limited automated matching accuracy, and therefore parent latent images must be retained with any extracted minutiae.

Additional Information/Guidance: NIST is conducting the Evaluation of Latent Fingerprints Technologies – Extended Feature Set (ELFT-EFS) to evaluate the accuracy of latent matching using features marked by experienced human latent fingerprint examiners. The EFS has been developed by the Committee to Define an Extended Fingerprint Feature Set (CDEFFS)[20] and will be an annex to ANSI/NIST-ITL.

---

[19] See section 14, page 36ff, of ANSI/NIST-ITL 1-2007, NIST Special Publication 500-271, http://fingerprint nist.gov/standard

[20] See http://fingerprint nist.gov/standard/cdeffs/ for the latest draft version of "Data Format for the Interchange of Extended Friction Ridge Features."

II.3.2   Two-Dimensional Face Images

There are a several standards for facial image data exchange. Facial images can be used for identification, identity verification, and credentialing. Many applications relate to travel documents and are therefore of interest to US-VISIT. Facial image data is stored in IDENT; however, there is currently no search or automated verification capability. Although DHS adopted ANSI INCITS 385-2004, Information technology – Face Recognition Format for Data Interchange,[21] for face recognition, conformance to the standard is not required for the submission of facial image data to US-VISIT at this time. US-VISIT will need to support each of the following standards and require that stakeholder face images be formatted in accordance with one of these standards: ANSI/NIST-ITL Type-10, ICAO 9303,[22] to support data exchange; and use of facial image data for both human and automated face recognition.

Table II-10. Two-Dimensional Face Images

Standard	Approved Use	US-VISIT Status	DHS TRM Category	Action Required
ICAO 9303	Capture and storage in MRTDs	Images captured by U.S. Citizenship and Immigration Services and Department of State comply with travel document standards. These images are available to IDENT.		Develop implementation plan
INCITS/ISO/IEC 19794-5:2005[2007], Full Frontal or Token	Storage of digital images in personal identity credentials	Not implemented	3.1.1.6-C	None
ANSI/NIST-ITL 1-2007 Type-10 with Subject Acquisition Profile (SAP) ≥ 10	Capture and storage (≥ 120 sec. capture acceptable)	Not implemented	1.4.4.2-A/1.4.4.3-C	None
INCITS/ISO/IEC 19794-5:2005[2007] Full Frontal or Token, with at least 90 pixels between the eyes[23]		Not implemented	3.1.1.6-C	None

---

[21] Department of Homeland Security Adopts Facial Recognition Standard, October 28, 2004. http://www.dhs.gov/xnews/releases/press_release_0550.shtm

[22] ICAO 9303 requires use of the ISO/IEC 19794-5 face image standard.

[23] SAP 13 and 14 will support use of ISO Full Frontal Facial Image and ISO Token Facial Image, respectively (INCITS/ISO/IEC 19794-5:2005[2007]). This approach could be used, for example, to communicate facial images obtained from e-passports.

Standard	Approved Use	US-VISIT Status	DHS TRM Category	Action Required
ANSI/NIST-ITL 2-2008 Type-10 with SAP ≥ 10	Capture and storage (≥ 120 sec. capture acceptable)	Not implemented		Develop implementation plan
ANSI/NIST-ITL 1-2007 Type-10 with SAP ≥ 1	Capture and storage (noncooperative or uncooperative)	Not implemented	1.4.4.2-A/1.4.4.3-C	None
INCITS/ISO/IEC 19794-5:2005 [2007], basic type only		Not implemented	3.1.1.6-C	None
ANSI/NIST-ITL 2-2008 Type-10 with SAP ≥ 1	Capture and storage (noncooperative or uncooperative	Not implemented		Develop implementation plan

No action is required for standards shown in gray text. These standards are included for completeness and possible future consideration.

Failure to require conformance to the requirements of these standards for image quality will undermine facial recognition performance. In 2008 US-VISIT conducted a technology assessment that automated image capture and performed real-time facial image quality assessment during the capture process. The prototype application code (integration of face finding and image quality software with camera software) that implements image quality checks is available for use by DHS and other agencies to help establish requirements for operational software development. US-VISIT should work with DHS customers to implement automated quality checks of facial images similar to the checks conducted for fingerprint quality.

ICAO Document 9303, Machine Readable Travel Documents, addresses the use of biometrics (face [primary biometric], fingerprint, and iris), contactless integrated circuit chips for data storage, a logical data (storage) structure, and data security based on public key infrastructure technology. This document is organized into three parts to address requirements for machine-readable passports, visas, and other official travel documents.

ICAO Document 9303 (Capture and Storage of Face Images in Machine-Readable Travel Documents)

Required Action:

- Implement support for face images in conformance with ICAO 9303.
- Develop a plan to implement ICAO 9303 in IXM.

US Registry Implementation Guidance:

- INCITS 385-2004 shall not be used.
- ANSI/NIST-ITL 1-2007 and ANSI/NIST-ITL 2-2008 shall not be used.

Additional Information/Guidance:

- Compatibility with international travel document standards is highly desirable.

- ICAO 9303 requires conformance with ISO/IEC 19794-5 full frontal or token for face image capture.
- ANSI/NIST-ITL Type-10 records support ISO/IEC 19794-5 images in Subject Acquisition Profiles (SAP) levels 13 and 14.

ANSI/NIST-ITL 2-2008 Type 10 (Capture and Storage of Face Images With SAP ≥ 10)

Required Action:

- Implement support for face image capture and storage (≥ 120 sec. capture acceptable) using ANSI/NIST-ITL 2-2008 Type-10 with SAP ≥ 10. The implementation plan will need to consider use cases and associated SAPs that require implementation.
- Develop a plan to implement ANSI/NIST-ITL 2-2008 Type-10 with SAP ≥ 10 in IXM.

US Registry Implementation Guidance:

- ISO/IEC 19794-5:2005, Amendment 1, should be consulted. It adds an annex to the base standard as guidance for producing either conventional printed photographs or digital images of faces that may be used in applications for passports, visas, or other identification documents.
- Data will need to conform, full frontal or token, with at least 90 pixels between the eyes from all subjects.

Additional Information/Guidance: None.

ANSI/NIST-ITL 2-2008 Type 10 (Capture and Storage of Face Images With SAP ≥ 1)

Required Action:

- Implement support for face image capture and storage (noncooperative or uncooperative) using ANSI/NIST-ITL 2-2008 Type-10 with SAP ≥ 1.
- Develop a plan to implement ANSI/NIST-ITL 2-2008 Type-10 with SAP ≥ 1 in IXM.

US Registry Implementation Guidance: None.

Additional Information/Guidance: None.

II.3.3   Iris Images

Plans are currently underway to implement iris recognition in US-VISIT systems. The following standards will be required to support this capability.

Table II-11. Iris Images

Standard	Approved Use	US-VISIT Status	DHS TRM Category	Action Required
ICAO 9303	Capture and storage in MRTDs	Not implemented		None
INCITS/ISO/IEC 19794-6:2005[2007] – rectilinear image format	Capture, storage, and exchange	Not implemented		None

Standard	Approved Use	US-VISIT Status	DHS TRM Category	Action Required
ANSI/NIST-ITL-1 2007, Type-17	Capture, storage, and exchange	Not implemented		Develop implementation plan
ANSI/NIST-ITL 2-2008 Type-17	Capture, storage, and exchange	Not implemented		Develop implementation plan

No action is required for standards shown in gray text. These standards are included for completeness and possible future consideration.

Lossy data compression must not be used. See the Iris Interoperability Exchange Test (IREX)[24] report.

ANSI/NIST-ITL-1 2007 Type-17

ANSI/NIST-ITL 2-2008 Type-17

Required Action:

- Develop a plan to implement ANSI/NIST-ITL 1-2007 Type-17 in IXM.
- Develop a plan to implement ANSI/NIST-ITL 2-2008 Type-17 in IXM.

US Registry Implementation Guidance: To achieve acceptable image quality, the compression ratio should not exceed 6:1.

Additional Information/Guidance:

- The use of JPEG2000 compression is recommended.
- The ANSI/NIST-ITL 1-2007 and 2-2008 Type-17 record formats are strict derivatives of INCITS/ISO/IEC 19794-6:2005[2007].

---

[24] http://iris.nist.gov/irex

III.   Biometric Transmission Profiles

US-VISIT provides biometric identification and identity analysis services that include biometric data storage, matching, analysis, and dissemination. As noted in section I, these services are provided to various stakeholders who use a number of formats and methods to exchange biometric data. Some of these formats and methods are nonstandard and are based on legacy systems and formats, while others use established national or international standards.

This section describes the transmission profiles currently used by US-VISIT and its primary stakeholders (section III.1), as well as the transmission profiles specifically required to achieve the end-state vision for US-VISIT systems (section III.2). Transmission between US-VISIT systems and some international biometric systems may also require accommodating legacy international standards as well as unique transaction requirements.

Transmission profiles define the sender and receiver specifications for electronic communications between systems, such as between US-VISIT and the FBI or between US-VISIT and a foreign government partner. For U.S. and many international biometric systems, most transmission profiles specify how the agency has implemented the ANSI/NIST-ITL standard for the exchange of biometric information via defined transaction types. The FBI's EBTS defines requirements for submitting requests to IAFIS; DOD's EBTS defines DOD-specific requirements for interfacing with its Automated Biometric Information System (ABIS); and US-VISIT IXM defines requirements for interfacing with IDENT.

III.1   Overview of Biometric Transmission Profiles

Transmission profiles and exchange standards currently used to share biometric information are summarized briefly in table III-1.

Table III-1. Overview of Biometric Transmission Profiles

Name	Description	Current Modalities	Stakeholders Currently Using Standard
IXM	XML framework for communication with US-VISIT systems; supports use of ANSI/NIST-ITL profiles via XML light wrapper (see section III.1.1)	Fingerprints (2 prints and 10 prints) and face data are also supported, but no standard for face has been implemented	Data sharing with US-VISIT stakeholders—CBP, DOS, and UKvisas—via direct implementation; other agencies, such as the FBI, via XML light wrapper
FBI EFTS v7.1	FBI implementation of ANSI/NIST-ITL 1-2000	Fingerprint, palmprint, face (mug shot), SMT	FBI; all State and local law enforcement agencies connecting with IAFIS; US-VISIT interface with IAFIS; DOS interface with IAFIS. All State and local internal networks that exchange biometric data and data exchange connectivity with other State and local agencies

Name	Description	Current Modalities	Stakeholders Currently Using Standard
FBI EBTS v8.1	FBI implementation of ANSI/NIST-ITL 1-2007	Fingerprint, palmprint, face, iris, other (Type-99), DNA flag field	Same as FBI EFTS v 7.1 as agencies migrate to this version
FBI EBTS v8.1 XML	XML implementation of EBTS v8.1	Fingerprint, palmprint, face, iris, other (Type-99), DNA flag field	FBI implementation pending
FBI EBTS v9.0	Update of FBI EBTS v8.1	Fingerprint, palmprint, face, iris, other (Type-99), DNA flag field	
FBI EBTS v9.0 XML	XML implementation of EBTS v9.0	Fingerprint, palmprint, face, iris, other (Type-99), DNA flag field	
DOD EBTS v1.2	DOD implementation of ANSI/NIST-ITL 1-2000	Fingerprint, palmprint, face (mug shot), SMT	Data sharing within DOD, between DOD and the FBI and the Intelligence Community
DOD EBTS v2.0	DOD implementation of ANSI/NIST-ITL 1-2007	Fingerprint, palmprint, face, iris, other (Type-99), DNA flag field	Data sharing within DOD, between DOD and the FBI and the Intelligence Community
INT-I v4.22b	Interpol implementation of ANSI/NIST-ITL 1-2000	Fingerprint, palmprint, face (mug shot), SMT	Data sharing in international community, via interface with FBI and DHS German Bundeskriminalamt (BKA) uses this version
INT-I v5.0	Interpol implementation of ANSI/NIST-ITL 1-2007	Fingerprint, palmprint, face, iris, other (Type-99), DNA flag field	Data sharing in international community, via interface with FBI and DHS
TWPDES v1.2b	Supports biographic and biometric data exchanges for watchlisting, person description, encounter management, and encounter management analysis	Biographic data only Face images	DHS, DOS, DOS, FBI, Intelligence Community Department of State

III.1.1   IDENT Exchange Messages (IXM)

The Automated Biometric Identification System (IDENT) Exchange Messages (IXM) Specification v3.1 is the transmission profile required for communicating with US-VISIT systems.[25] It establishes common interface specifications and mechanisms for new US-VISIT systems users; leverages existing data models and standards, such as ANSI/NIST-ITL 1-2007, FBI EFTS v7.1, and FBI EBTS v8.1; and leverages existing Web service specifications and technology for binary data transmission.

---

[25] Automated Biometric Identification System (IDENT) Exchange Messages (IXM) Specification v3.1, DHS/US-VISIT, November 26, 2008; http://www.biometrics.gov/Standards/IXM_Spec_3_1.pdf

IXM offers two methods for transferring data: (1) embedding an ANSI/NIST-ITL record in a lightweight XML wrapper and (2) encoding data directly in XML (also known as pure XML). The lightweight XML wrapper maintains the structure of the embedded ANSI/NIST-ITL record and its tagged field format data is parsed and processed by US-VISIT systems. The pure XML method allows a more direct interpretation of the data and accommodates greater flexibility for data definitions.

III.1.2   FBI EFTS and FBI EBTS

FBI EFTS v7.1, the FBI application profile of ANSI/NIST-ITL 1-2000, and FBI EBTS v8.1 and v9.0,[26] the FBI application profiles of ANSI/NIST-ITL 1-2007, define the specifications to which agencies must adhere when electronically communicating with the FBI's IAFIS. They provide descriptions of all requests and responses associated with electronic fingerprint identification services, including 10-print, latent, and fingerprint image services. FBI EBTS v9.0 includes sections that will be developed further to address future FBI capabilities, such as palmprint, face, and iris matching.

With the development of Next Generation Identification (NGI) by the FBI's Criminal Justice Information Services (CJIS) Division, the FBI EBTS v9.0 has been reorganized into user services that include:[27]

- Identification Service
- Verification Service
- Information Service
- Investigation Service
- Notification Service
- Data Management Service

III.1.3   DOD EBTS

DOD EBTS v1.2 describes customizations of FBI EFTS v7.0 transactions that are necessary to utilize the DOD ABIS, which was designed to be similar to the FBI's IAFIS. The ABIS interface was therefore based on the FBI EFTS. Because of the different nature of DOD encounters and detainment circumstances, DOD has additional operational requirements beyond those defined in the FBI EFTS, which are defined in the DOD EBTS v1.2.

DOD EBTS v2.0 is an application profile of ANSI/NIST-ITL 1-2007 that builds upon the base standard to meet DOD requirements. DOD EBTS v2.0 employs data elements defined in the DOD Integrated Data Dictionary. Definitions for transactions are provided in DOD application-specific documents, which list the quantities necessary for each logical record for a particular transaction. These documents also identify mandatory and optional fields for the transactions.

---

[26] See http://www.fbibiospecs.org/docs/EBTS_v9_0_User_Services_Final_11_30_2009.pdf (EBTS v9.0, tagged fields) and http://www.fbibiospecs.org/ebts_v9_xml html (EBTS v9.0 XML versions).

[27] Currently, CJIS IAFIS has six segments; see Section 1.2 of EBTS v9.0, http://www.fbibiospecs.org/docs/EBTS_v9_0_User_Services_Final_11_30_2009.pdf

III.1.4   Interpol Implementation (INT-I)

The Interpol Implementation (INT-I) was written to supplement the ANSI/NIST-ITL standard for the guidance of members of Interpol. INT-I was agreed to by all Interpol member countries as the standard for fingerprint exchange. Records described in INT-I are not intended for manual entry and interpretation; they are intended for the transmission of information between computers.[28, 29] INT-I v4.22b is an application profile of ANSI/NIST-ITL 1-2000. INT-I v5.0 is an application profile of ANSI/NIST 1-2007.

III.1.5   Terrorist Watchlist Person Data Exchange Standard (TWPDES)

The Terrorist Watchlist Person Data Exchange Standard (TWPDES)[30] is an XML standard that supports biographic and biometric data exchanges for watchlisting, person description, encounter management, and encounter management analysis. It is in conformance with the National Information Exchange Model (NIEM) v2.0 and incorporates the Information Sharing Environment – Suspicious Activity Reporting (ISE-SAR) Functional Standard[31] and the Logical Entity Exchange Specifications (LEXS).[32] Several interagency partners exchange biographic data by means of TWPDES, and the Terrorist Screening Center and the Department of State exchange face images by means of TWPDES.

In compliance with the strategic roadmap required by the Executive Order (EO) 13356, the Central Intelligence Agency (CIA), National Counterterrorism Center (NCTC), Terrorist Screening Center (TSC), FBI, and Office of Justice Programs (OJP) harmonized the original TWPDES with the Global Justice XML Data Model (GJXDM) person and other classes to produce the Common Terrorism Information Sharing Standards (CTISS[33]) version. This effort was also required by Presidential Memorandum ISE-ANI-300. A harmonization effort for data exchange between TSC and the FBI systems is currently under way. This effort is expected to result in a recommendation on the final data interchange format.

III.2   Biometric Transmission Profiles Required for US-VISIT Systems

IDENT exchange messages (IXM) is the US-VISIT transmission profile required for communicating with US-VISIT systems. Currently, IXM supports the FBI EBTS v8.1 and EFTS v7.1 transmission profiles, which are compliant with the ANSI/NIST-ITL-1-2007 and ANSI/NIST-ITL 1-2000 standards (see table III-2 below). At a high level, this support includes the following aspects:

---

[28] See http://www.interpol.int/Public/Forensic/fingerprints/RefDoc/implementation6.pdf

[29] See http://www.interpol.int/Public/Forensic/fingerprints/RefDoc/implementation7.pdf

[30] See http://www.niem.gov/TWPDES.php

[31] See http://www.ise.gov/pages/sar-initiative.html

[32] See http://www.lexs.gov

[33] See http://www.fas.org/irp/agency/ise/ctiss.pdf

- The fingerprint and face data biometric exchange formats implemented in IXM are equivalent to those implemented in FBI EBTS v8.1.
- US-VISIT IXM implementation can accept FBI EBTS v8.1 and earlier EFTS version records when a stakeholder "wraps" the data records in XML code specified by US-VISIT.

As shown in table III-2, US-VISIT currently addresses a number of standards with variations within these standards to accommodate legacy applications. At the same time, US-VISIT needs to provide interoperability with additional partners who have implemented the ANSI/NIST-ITL standard to meet their mission and application needs, and to accommodate the use of new modalities. Furthermore, US-VISIT should initiate automation of the current manual data exchange processes. The use of special processes should be reduced and greater standardization should be implemented within US-VISIT systems. Lastly, many stakeholders have already indicated that they are planning to move to an XML implementation of the ANSI/NIST-ITL standard for communication with their biometric systems.

Analysis of the biometric standards and approaches currently used by US-VISIT and its stakeholders shows that there is significant commonality. Considerable interagency work is under way by DOJ/FBI, DOD, DHS, DOS, and NIST to harmonize biometric and biographic data exchanges using NIEM-conforming messages encoded in XML. All planned conversion must consider the need for conformance with, or backward compatibility to, the ANSI/NIST-ITL tagged-field standard. Because the ANSI/NIST-ITL set of standards is so firmly established in the national and international communities, it must continue to play a key part in the end-state vision.

Differences between the various implementations of the ANSI/NIST-ITL standards may diminish as part of the ongoing coordination process being conducted by stakeholders. However, it is likely that some differences will not be resolved since law enforcement, immigration and border management, and military agencies have different missions and need different information about a subject and circumstances surrounding the collection of biometric data. Furthermore, new applications and new modalities may result in additional variations. Therefore, an end-state vision for US-VISIT interoperability has been established as follows:

- US-VISIT will continue to maintain and expand the use of IXM for all new customers and modalities that do not currently use an ANSI/NIST-based exchange standard. New applications that are not already in ANSI/NIST format will be implemented directly in IXM.
- US-VISIT will accept and process data in ANSI/NIST-ITL 2-2008 and its application profiles (all in XML) for those applications that are currently using or that have historically used an ANSI/NIST based standard. All applications currently accepted in legacy ANSI/NIST format will be in ANSI/NIST-ITL 2-2008.
  - o A remap of the various ANSI/NIST-based standards (FBI EBTS, DOD EBTS, and Interpol) will be used to achieve data compatibility.
  - o IXM will use data specifications (fingerprint size, resolution, etc.) as specified in ANSI/NIST-ITL 2-2008 as a default specification.
- Manual processing will be eliminated or at least minimized.
- IXM will be in conformance with ANSI/NIST-ITL 2-2008.

Table III-2 shows the current and expected future methods for data exchange for US-VISIT principal stakeholders.

Table III-2. Current and Expected Future Methods[34] of Data Exchange with US-VISIT

US-VISIT Interoperability Stakeholders	Current Method of Data Exchange	Expected Future Method of Data Exchange	Type of Data
DHS – CBP	IXM using pure XML	IXM using pure XML	Current: Face image, 10-print, and 4-print images, 6-finger minutiae (index, middle, ring) in matcher vendor format Future: Face image, 10-print, and 4-print images; 6-finger minutiae (index, middle, ring) in matcher vendor format, palmprint data, iris image, DNA (in EBTS v9.0 compatible format)
DHS – CIS	IXM using XML lightly wrapped FBI EBTS v8.1	XML FBI EBTS v9.0	Current: 10-print images Future: 10-print images, face image
DHS – TSA	Manual process	IXM using pure XML	Current: 10-print images Future: 10-print images, face image
DHS – Coast Guard	IXM using XML lightly wrapped FBI EBTS v8.1 as modified to accommodate 2-finger transmission	XML FBI EBTS v9.0	Current: 2-print images and face image Future: 2-print images, face image, iris image
FBI	IAFIS: IXM using XML lightly wrapped FBI EBTS v8.1	NGI: XML FBI EBTS v9.0	Current: 10-print images Future: 10-print and latent fingerprint data, face image, iris image, palmprint data, DNA
DOD ABIS	Fingerprint data sent via e-mail and search and enrolls are processed manually	XML DOD EBTS	Current: 2-print images Future: 10-print and latent fingerprint data, palmprint data, face image, iris image, DNA
DOS	IXM using pure XML	IXM using pure XML	Current: Face image, 10-print images Future: 10-print images, face image, iris image

---

[34] Expected Future Methods of Data Exchange are based on current trends for these organizations; that is, the expected methods are based on what these organizations are planning as of this writing.

US-VISIT Interoperability Stakeholders	Current Method of Data Exchange	Expected Future Method of Data Exchange	Type of Data
TSC	Manual process to accommodate TWPDES v1.2b[35]	To be determined	Current: Biographic data only Future: 10-print and latent fingerprint data, face image, iris image
DHS – BSC	Manual process	XML FBI EBTS v9.0	Current: Encoded latent fingerprints to IDENT via custom process Future: Image and encoded latent fingerprints to IDENT via custom and standardized processes
Interpol	Submissions go through a legacy interface provided by US-VISIT and are formatted by the matcher vendor INT-I as modified to accommodate 2-finger transmission	XML INT-I v (future XML implementation)	Current: 2 print images Future: 10-print and latent fingerprint data, face image
UKvisas	IXM using pure XML	IXM using pure XML	Current: 2-print images Future: 10-print data, face image
Federal Criminal Police Office of Germany (BKA)	None	INT-I v4.22b	Current: None Future: 10-print and latent fingerprints, palmprints
State and local law enforcement (Secure Communities)	FBI EBTS v8.1 submitted to FBI for forwarding to US-VISIT (see FBI IAFIS) Responses are returned to State/local via the DHS Law Enforcement Support Center	FBI to continue forwarding to US-VISIT	Current: 2-print images Future: 10-print images, face image
Five Country Conference (FCC)	SFTP from Australian server	To be determined	Current: None Future: 10-print image

Addressing XML-based differences, such as those between the FBI EBTS XML implementation and the DOD EBTS XML implementation, will be much simpler than the current remapping from binary tagged field data to IXM's XML implementation.

---

[35] TWPDES v1.2b is based on FBI EBTS v8.1 XML.

The diversity of transmission profiles and standards is due in part to the fact that the systems were implemented at different times and were intended to address the different mission requirements of Federal, State, and local law enforcement, military applications, and international police action; and in some cases because the standards available at the time were not sufficiently developed or have been updated since the original system implementation.

In addition, there are a number of significant differences in how stakeholders have implemented a particular standard for interoperability with US-VISIT systems. These differences vary in type; for example, differences in transaction types, domain names, biographic data elements (ANSI/NIST Type-2 record differences), and image data specifications.

III.3   XML Implementation

IXM v3.1 is not directly compatible with ANSI/NIST-ITL 2-2008 or ANSI/NIST-ITL 2-2008 profiles, such as the FBI EBTS v8.1 (and newer versions) XML Information Exchange Package (IEPD). To achieve compatibility, US-VISIT will modify IXM and remap to the IXM schema as required. Backward compatibility must be maintained with all data formats currently accepted by US-VISIT until those formats are phased out.

All mapping schemes should provide compatibility between the IDENT- (IXM-) recognized data and stakeholder data. Only fields (data) required for processing a service request by IDENT need to be addressed. Transactions, domain names, and Type-2 data not used by IDENT can be ignored. An example of the current remapping scheme for IXM to EFTS is provided in appendix C of the IXM specification,[36] version 3.1.

III.4   Actions Required to Facilitate System Interoperability

This section provides a description of the actions required to facilitate interoperability between US-VISIT's systems and its stakeholders. Also addressed are high-level activities that are necessary for strategic planning and coordination among various stakeholders.

IDENT Exchange Messages (IXM)

Required Action:

- US-VISIT should continue to maintain IXM and update as needed to support new business requirements and interoperability at a minimum with the FBI (EBTS), DOD (EBTS), the National Terrorist Screening Center (NTSC, TWPDES), and Interpol (INT-I).
- Considerable interagency (DOJ/FBI, DOD, DHS, DOS, NIST) work is under way to harmonize biometric and biographic data exchanges using NIEM-compliant messages encoded in XML. US-VISIT should participate in these activities and update IXM accordingly once an approach has been finalized. US-VISIT should actively pursue the harmonization of data for exchange with international agencies.

---

[36] http://www.biometrics.gov/Standards/default.aspx

TWPDES 1.2b

Required Action: Considerable interagency (DOJ/FBI, DOD, DHS, DOS, NIST) work is under way to harmonize biometric and biographic data exchanges using NIEM-compliant messages encoded in XML. US-VISIT should participate in these activities and update IXM accordingly once an approach has been finalized

FBI EFTS v7.1, EBTS v8.1, EBTS v9.0

Required Action:

- EFTS v7.1 – No specific action required. EFTS v7.1 has been superseded by EBTS v8.1. IXM can already accept EFTS v7.1 data that contains an IXM XML wrapper.
- EBTS v8.1 and v8.1 XML – No specific action required. IXM can already accept EFTS v7.1 data that contains an IXM XML wrapper. EBTS v8.1 offers a superset of the functionality provided by prior versions (e.g., EFTS).and is backward compatible with prior versions.
- EBTS v9.0 and v9.0 XML –EBTS v9.0 was released effective November 30, 2009 (http://www.fbibiospecs.org/docs/EBTS_v9_0_User_Services_Final_11_30_2009.pdf). EBTS v9.0 offers a superset of the functionality provided by prior versions and is backward compatible with prior versions. US-VISIT should develop the capability to accept EBTS v9.0 XML messages directly.

DOD EBTS v1.2 and v2.0

Required Action:

- Interagency (DOJ/FBI, DOD, DHS, DOS, NIST) work is under way to harmonize biometric and biographic data exchanges using NIEM-compliant messages encoded in XML. US-VISIT should participate in these activities.
- US-VISIT is engaging DOD in a DOD-DHS Interoperability IPT. US-VISIT should update IXM accordingly once an overall approach has been finalized.
- DOD EBTS v1.2 offers a superset of the functionality provided by FBI EFTS v7.1 for DOD-specific applications. The FBI is currently considering implementation of this functionality into the FBI EBTS. US-VISIT should monitor and participate in related activities.
- US-VISIT should support activities leading to the development of an XML version of DOD EBTS. Once such a profile is finalized, US-VISIT should develop the capability to accept DOD EBTS XML messages directly.

Interpol Implementation of ANSI/NIST-ITL 1-2000 v4.22b (INT I)

Required Action:

- To accommodate the data-sharing agreement that has been developed with Germany, US-VISIT will need to accommodate INT-I v4.22b, which is the transmission profile currently used by Germany. US-VISIT will need to reconcile the XML schema provided by Germany for requests and responses with the IXM wrapper for data records.
- While US-VISIT already accepts FBI EFTS and EBTS records that are wrapped in XML, US-VISIT will need to examine the Type-2 data field assignments in INT-I v4.22b and remap those fields that do not align with the existing IXM implementation.

Interpol Implementation of ANSI/NIST-ITL 1-2007 v5.00 (INT-I)

Required Action:

- While US-VISIT already accepts ANSI/NIST-ITL 1-2007 records that are wrapped appropriately in XML, US-VISIT will need to examine the Type-2 data field assignments in INT-I v5.00 and remap those fields that do not align precisely with an existing IXM implementation.
- Monitor Interpol activities with respect to the potential development of an XML version of the standard.

IV.   Related Standards and Guidance

To achieve data exchange interoperability with other biometric systems, IXM will be expanded to provide compatibility with transmission profiles used by DOD, TSC, and Interpol. Each of these profiles is based on the ANSI/NIST-ITL standards, and the differences between the profiles are readily accommodated. A global translator is being developed to allow direct communication between US-VISIT and its national and international partners using IXM and a limited number of widely used transmission profiles.

Interoperability also requires compatibility in data quality. Data quality is standardized using image quality standards such as the NFIQ and fingerprint image compression standards such as WSQ or JPEG-2000. To ensure full interoperability with both Federal and international systems, US-VISIT must maintain awareness of the approaches taken by other Federal agencies to establish quality standards and establish data quality standards for US-VISIT systems. The data quality metrics associated with such standards must be used to ensure that only biometric data samples of a minimum quality are stored in IDENT. Quality metrics can also be used to optimize biometric matching on a sample-by-sample basis.

The international biometric standards development organization (JTC 1/ SC 37) has developed a framework that –

1. Establishes terms and definitions that are useful in the specification and use of quality metrics

2. Recommends the purpose and interpretation of biometric quality scores

3. Defines the format and placement of quality data fields in biometric data exchange and storage formats

4. Suggests methods for developing biometric sample datasets for the purpose of quality score normalization

5. Suggests the format for exchanging quality algorithm results

In addition to the framework, there are technical reports that define and specify methodologies for computing objective, quantitative quality scores for finger images and face images. Work to define and specify methodologies for the computation of objective, quantitative quality scores for iris images is ongoing. Future versions of this document will include additional information on the data quality standards applicable to US-VISIT systems.

Performance Testing: Performance testing measures one or more characteristics of a biometric component (e.g., device, subsystem, or system), including accuracy, speed, throughput, and usability under various conditions. Technology, scenario, and operational performance tests may be conducted based on established testing methodologies and metrics. Future versions of this document will include additional information on performance testing standards applicable to US-VISIT systems.

IV.1   FBI "Appendix F"

US-VISIT requires that all fingerprint capture devices conform with the FBI EFTS and FBI EBTS, Appendix F, IAFIS Image Quality Specifications. Appendix F identifies the criteria for ensuring the image quality of fingerprint scanners that input fingerprint images to US-VISIT and

IAFIS, and printers that generate hardcopies of fingerprint images. The specification defines the quality characteristics of fingerprint images, including the resolution range, preferred size, linearity, geometric accuracy, spatial frequency response, signal-to-noise ratio, gray-level uniformity, and gray-scale dynamic range. Scanners designed for "Identification Flats," sets of plain impressions that will be applied to US-VISIT, must meet additional requirements (also defined in appendix F) for verifiable finger sequencing, requiring the capture of four fingers simultaneously in an upright position.

US-VISIT accepts data from devices that capture rolled or plain impressions (flats) or both types of data. The FBI maintains a list of fingerprint scanners that have been certified to be in conformance with the image quality specification. To achieve the expected levels of search accuracy, all fingerprint data must be captured on devices that are certified by the FBI.[37] This standard is currently used by US-VISIT and its stakeholders and no changes are expected at this time.

IV.2   FBI Wavelet Scalar Quantization

The Wavelet Scalar Quantization (WSQ) Gray-Scale Fingerprint Image Compression Algorithm is the standard for exchanging fingerprint images within the criminal justice community. It specifies the class of encoders required for converting source fingerprint image data to compressed image data, the decoder process for converting compressed image data to reconstructed fingerprint image data, and the coded representations for compressed image data with minimal loss of information.

The transmission of 500 pixels/inch fingerprint images to US-VISIT already are and will continue to be compressed using the WSQ compression specification. EFTS also requires WSQ compression when submitting fingerprint images to IAFIS, and specifies a compression ratio of 15-to-1. This standard is currently used by US-VISIT and its stakeholders and no changes are expected at this time.

IV.3   JPEG for Facial Images

The term Joint Photographic Experts Group (JPEG) refers to the international standard ("Digital Compression and Coding of Continuous-Tone Still Images," ISO/IEC 10918) from the JPEG committee (http://www.jpeg.org) that defines the method for compressing still images of photographic quality. JPEG is designed for compressing full-color or gray-scale images of natural, real-world scenes. It works well on photographs, naturalistic artwork, and similar material, but not so well on lettering, simple cartoons, or line drawings. JPEG handles only still images.

The JPEG File Interchange Format (JFIF) specifies a file format that enables the exchange of JPEG compressed images.

Face images captured by U.S. Customs and Border Protection are currently compressed using JPEG compression before being transmitted to US-VISIT. The FBI EFTS also allows JPEG

---

[37] See the certified product list at http://www.fbibiospecs.org/IAFIS/Default.aspx

compression when submitting facial and SMT images to IAFIS; however, it should be noted that at the ANSI/NIST Fingerprint Standard Update Workshop II in December 2005, JPEG 2000 was declared the preference over JPEG.

IV.4   JPEG 2000

The JPEG 2000 Image Coding System is the latest series of standards (ISO/IEC 15444) from the JPEG committee. JPEG 2000 uses wavelet technology to compress images, allowing an image to be retained without any distortion or loss. Specifically, the series of standards define a set of lossless (bit-preserving) and lossy compression methods for coding continuous-tone, bilevel, gray-scale, or color digital still images. It specifies the encoding process for converting source image data to compressed image data, the decoding processes for converting compressed image data to reconstructed image data, and a file format for storing compressed image data.

JPEG 2000 has the potential for use by US-VISIT, replacing the use of the original JPEG standard. There are two initiatives that affect the adoption of JPEG 2000 by US-VISIT:

- As noted above, the ANSI/NIST Fingerprint Standard Workshop II recently approved the use of JPEG 2000 compressed images in favor of JPEG compressed images for representing facial and SMT information. JPEG compressed images are still allowed for backward compatibility reasons. It is unknown if EFTS will also adopt this compression method.
- The FBI has adopted a JPEG 2000 profile for 1000 pixel per inch (ppi) fingerprint images, as the WSQ algorithm did not function as expected when applied to these higher resolution images. This profile is a restricted subset of JPEG 2000 parameter settings to ensure image quality and interoperability. It also provides a path for transcoding 1000 ppi JPEG 2000 images to 500 ppi WSQ images. Use of JPEG 2000 with the 1000 ppi profile will be included in EBTS. (WSQ compression is still required for 500 ppi fingerprint images.)

The use of JPEG 2000 may also have future benefit for US-VISIT if facial recognition technology is integrated into the system, as JPEG 2000 provides better image quality than traditional JPEG at a fixed compression rate. The use of JPEG 2000 as a replacement for JPEG for use with facial images should be studied further.

IV.5   NFIQ Fingerprint Image Quality Standard

The NIST Fingerprint Image Quality (NFIQ) value is a prediction of a matcher's performance, reflecting the positive or negative contribution of an individual sample to the overall performance of a fingerprint-matching system. It consists of five levels of quality related to the performance of a minutiae-based fingerprint-matching system. An NFIQ of 1 indicates high-quality samples and 5 indicates poor sample quality.

The NIST NFIQ algorithm performs a feature extraction operation followed by a neural network that assesses quality based on a normalized score distribution. It has been shown to accurately predict matching performance across a variety of datasets and matching algorithms.

NFIQ has been adopted by the FBI EFTS, and therefore is becoming the de facto standard algorithm for measuring fingerprint quality. NFIQ is publicly available, subject to export restrictions, and is documented in NIST Internal Report (NISTIR) 7151.

Fingerprint image quality assessment is a critical element of the US-VISIT system since image quality has a direct effect on subsequent fingerprint-matching performance. Quality feedback is important during enrollment to allow for recapture and during subsequent operations to allow for the comparison of samples for selection/retention purposes.

The NFIQ is modality-specific and applies only to minutiae-based fingerprint matchers. It should also be noted that the quality range specified in the NFIQ (i.e., 1–5) is different than how quality is represented within INCITS and ISO standards (e.g., BioAPI, CBEFF, and data format standards), which use a range of 1–100, with qualitative assessments (i.e., unacceptable, marginal, adequate, or excellent) being assigned to quartiles. However, the numeric values are linearly translatable.

The NFIQ standard is useful for helping the operator to assess that the image capture quality is as good as possible.

This standard is not a requirement, but US-VISIT recommends its use by US-VISIT stakeholders. Because image quality standards are being improved, US-VISIT should periodically assess the state of the practice and the development of new image quality standards.

IV.6   Other Image Quality Standards

Significant development work is occurring in this technology area. DOD and other agencies are researching algorithms that may be used to determine quality scores of two-dimensional frontal-view face images and iris images.

DOD is also currently developing a tool to determine quality measurement values for finger images. The Fingerprint Image Quality Measurement (FIQM) toolset is a fingerprint quality measurement tool based on an algorithm that models the human perception of quality. This tool is optimized for determining fingerprint image quality as it would be determined by a human examiner. The method first identifies the fingerprint image's region of interest (ROI) and then targets that area for quality measurement. The quality level is determined by the majority orientation within local areas. An image's overall single quality score is calculated by taking the average of all the local areas' quality levels. The FIQM returns a single score to represent the image quality level, which can be a number from 0 (poor) to 100 (excellent).

Because image quality standards are being improved, US-VISIT should periodically assess the state of the practice and the development of new image quality standards.

IV.7   NIST SP 500-280

NIST announced the release of Special Publication 500-280, Mobile ID Device Best Practices Recommendation Version 1.0,[38] in August 2009. SP 500-280 provides guidance and operational requirements for mobile identification devices that can be used for enrollment, identification, and verification functions. It also provides guidelines to promote the interoperability of such devices

---

[38] See http://fingerprint.nist.gov/mobileid/MobileID-BPRS-20090825-V100.pdf, published August 25, 2009.

with each other as well as with legacy systems. This guidance document will likely become a de facto standard that will be used by DHS, FBI, and DOD.

Information is to be captured, compiled, and formatted in accordance with SP 500-280 and is to be compliant with the target system's implementation of ANSI/NIST-ITL 1-2007 or ANSI/NIST-ITL 2-2008. This data can be transmitted and seamlessly exchanged by most of the biometric systems.

For systems based on or requiring connectivity with the FBI, these profiles will rely on the FBI's current version of the EBTS in addition to the ANSI/NIST-ITL standards. EBTS specifies record types with field requirements that are based on existing and planned systems. For connectivity with non-EBTS based systems, the profiles must be compliant with the target system's domain-specific EBTS.

Captured images containing more than a single finger must use the ANSI/NIST-ITL Type-14 record in order to specify the segmentation coordinates for each finger. The system should use the NFIQ algorithm and should alert the operator if a poor fingerprint image was captured (NFIQ level 4 or 5).

For the exchange of facial images, the ANSI/NIST-ITL 1-2007 Type-10 logical record must be used to encode compressed-image files and other metadata. The mobile identification face capture device must be able to measure face image quality or to provide some means by which the device operator can assess the quality of the captured face image. In order to support interoperability, the Mobile ID iris image capture device shall support ANSI/NIST-ITL Type-17 records, with raw images in conformance with ISO 19794-6 rectilinear image standards.

V.   Standards for Future Consideration

The following standards are currently not implemented by US-VISIT. They have been identified as part of the US-VISIT Technical Reference Architecture and as such will provide a potential migration standard for any future implementation.

V.1   Biometric Data, Collection, Storage, and Exchange Standards

V.1.1   DNA Identification

The FBI exchanges deoxyribonucleic acid (DNA) data with State and local law enforcement agencies and the international community and maintains the data in the National DNA Index System (NDIS).[39] It uses a common message format (CMF), implemented by vendors of genetic analyzers, analytical software, etc., for interoperability with the Combined DNA Index System (CODIS) database. CMF Version 1 supports storing DNA data, Version 3.2 provides an XML message capability, and Version 4.1 supports data exchange of mitochondrial DNA data in XML. Interpol also operates a "DNA Gateway" for data sharing among 29 countries.

The FBI, together with the international community, is supporting the development of a new standard to be called ISO/IEC 19794 Biometric Data Interchange Formats Part 14 – DNA Data. The standard approval process is expected to be completed by November 17, 2011, and final publication will occur by May 17, 2012.

US-VISIT should become engaged in the standard development process and plans for its implantation should be developed. A draft standard is available for comment and planning.

V.1.2   Speaker Identification

This section is reserved for future use.

V.2   Biometric Identity Credentialing Profiles

This section is reserved for future use.

V.3   Biometric Technical Interface Standards

This section is reserved for future use.

V.3.1   Biometric Application Programming Interface (BioAPI)

This section is reserved for future use.

---

[39] See http://www.dna.gov/dna-databases/levels.

Table V-1. Biometric Application Programming Interface (BioAPI)

Standard	Approved Use	US-VISIT Status	DHS TRM Category	Action Required
INCITS/ISO/IEC 19784-1:2006[2007]		Not implemented		None
INCITS/ISO/IEC 19784-2:2007[2008]		Not implemented		None
INCITS 358:2002		Not implemented		None

V.3.2   Common Biometric Exchange File Format (CBEFF)

This section is reserved for future use.

Table V-2. Common Biometric Exchange File Format (CBEFF)

Standard	Approved Use	US-VISIT Status	DHS TRM Category	Action Required
INCITS 398:2008		Not implemented		None

V.3.3   Biometric Identity Assurance Services (BIAS)

This section is reserved for future use.

Table V-3. Biometric Identity Assurance Services (BIAS)

Standard	Approved Use	US-VISIT Status	DHS TRM Category	Action Required
INCITS 442:2008		Not implemented		Investigate need for implementation

V.4   Biometric Conformance Testing Methodology Standards

This section is reserved for future use.

V.5   Biometric Performance Testing Methodology Standards

This section is reserved for future use.

V.6   ISO/IEC 15948 Format (Portable Network Graphics)

This section is reserved for future use.

V.7   International Committee for Information Technology Standards (INCITS) 394-2004: Application Profile – Biometrics at the Border

This standard specifies the application profile to be used when incorporating biometrically based identification and verification into border management applications and systems. Border management includes prearrival, arrival, stay management, departure, and database reconciliation/management. DHS components have implemented biometric standards to meet their operational needs and do not subscribe to the application profile. Therefore, DHS has requested that INCITS 394, Information Technology Application Profile for Interoperability, Data Interchange, and Data Integrity of Biometric-Based Personal Identification for Border Management, be withdrawn. It should not be included in any future plans by US-VISIT.

VI.   Referenced Documents

Department of Defense:

http://www.biometrics.dod.mil/CurrentInitiatives/Standards/dodebts.aspx

- "Electronic Biometric Transmission Specification (EBTS)," Version 1.2, November 8, 2006.
  http://www.biometrics.dod.mil/Files/Documents/Standards/DOD_BTF_TS_EBTS_Nov06_01%2002%2000.pdf
- "Electronic Biometric Transmission Specification (EBTS)," Version 2.0, March 27, 2009.
  http://www.biometrics.dod.mil/Files/Documents/Standards/DOD_ABIS_EBTS_v2.0.pdf

Department of Homeland Security/US-VISIT:

- Automated Biometric Identification System (IDENT) Exchange Messages (IXM) Specification – v3.1, DHS/US-VISIT, November 26, 2008.
  http://www.biometrics.gov/Standards/IXM_Spec_3_1.pdf

Department of Justice:

http://www.fbibiospecs.org

- "Electronic Fingerprint Transmission Specification (EFTS)," Version 7.1, May 2, 2005 (IAFIS-DOC-01078-7), Federal Bureau of Investigation, Criminal Justice Information Services Division. http://www.fbi.gov/hq/cjisd/iafis/efts71/efts71.pdf
- "Electronic Biometric Transmission Specification (EBTS)," Version 8.1, May 2, 2009 (IAFIS-DOC-01078-7), Federal Bureau of Investigation, Criminal Justice Information Services Division. http://www.fbibiospecs.org/fbibiometric/biospecs.html
- EBTS Version 9.0, November 30, 2009, IAFIS-DO-01078-9.0 under DOJ entries.
  http://www.fbibiospecs.org/ebts.html
- "Global Justice XML Data Model (GJXDM)," Version 3.0.3, August 2005, Department of Justice, Office of Justice Programs. http://www.it.ojp.gov/gjxdm
- Wavelet Scalar Quantization (WSQ) Gray-Scale Fingerprint Image Compression Algorithm. http://fingerprint.nist.gov/wsq

International Civil Aviation Organization (ICAO):

http://www2.icao.int/en/mrtd/Pages/default.aspx

- ICAO Doc 9303, "Machine Readable Travel Documents," Part 1 – Machine Readable Passport, Volume 2, Specifications for Electronically Enabled Passports with Biometric Identification Capabilities, 6th edition, 2006.
  http://www2.icao.int/en/MRTD/Downloads/Doc%209303
- Supplement to Doc 9303, Release 7, November 19, 2008.
  http://www2.icao.int/en/MRTD/Downloads/Supplements%20to%20Doc%209303/Supplement%20to%20ICAO%20Doc%209303%20-%20Release%207.pdf

InterNational Committee for Information Technology Standards (INCITS) M1 Biometrics:

https://m1.incits.org

International Standards Organization/International Electrotechnical Commission Joint Technical Committee 1/Subcommittee 37, Biometrics:

http://isotc.iso.org/livelink/livelink?func=ll&objId=2262372&objAction=browse&sort=name

Interpol:

http://www.interpol.int/Public/Forensic/Fingerprints/Default.asp

- ANSI/NIST-ITL 1-2000 Date Format for the Interchange of Fingerprint, Facial & SMT Information Interpol Implementation, Version 4.22b – October 28, 2005 http://www.interpol.int/Public/Forensic/fingerprints/RefDoc/implementation6.pdf
- ANSI/NIST-ITL 1-2000 Date Format for the Interchange of Fingerprint, Facial & SMT Information Interpol Implementation, Version 5.0 – October 23, 2008 http://www.interpol.int/Public/Forensic/fingerprints/RefDoc/implementation7.pdf

National Institute of Standards and Technology (NIST):

http://www.nist.gov/index.html

- ANSI/NIST-ITL 1-2007, "Data Format for the Interchange of Fingerprint, Facial, & Other Biometric Information," April 20, 2007 (ANSI/NIST-ITL 1-2007/NIST Special Publication 500-271). http://biometrics.nist.gov/standard
- ANSI/NIST-ITL 2-2008, Data Format for the Interchange of Fingerprint, Facial, & Other Biometric Information – Part 2: XML Version, August 12, 2008. http://biometrics.nist.gov/standard
- "Fingerprint Image Quality," August 19, 2004 (NISTIR 7151). http://fingerprint.nist.gov/NFIS/ir_7151.pdf
- IREX I Performance of Iris Recognition Algorithms on Standard Images NIST Interagency Report 7629. http://iris.nist.gov/irex

National Science and Technology Council (NSTC) Subcommittee on Biometrics and Identity Management (SCA):

- Registry of USG Recommended Biometric Standards, Version 2.0, August 10, 2009. http://www.biometrics.gov/Standards/Biometric_Standards_Registr y_v2.pdf

Organization for the Advancement of Structured Information Standards (OASIS):

http://www.oasis-open.org/committees/bias/faq.php

- ANSI/INCITS 442-2008, Information Technology Services – Biometric Identity Assurance Services (BIAS), May 21, 2008.

Other

- "National Information Exchange Model (NIEM)," Version 0.2.1, February 24, 2006, Departments of Homeland Security and Justice. http://www.niem.gov
- JPEG 2000 standard, http://www.jpeg.org/jpeg/index.html
- JPEG 2000 series of standards, http://www.jpeg.org/jpeg2000/index.html

VII.   Abbreviations and Acronyms

ABIS	Automated Biometric Identification System
AFIS	Automated Fingerprint Identification System
AMD	Amendment
ANSI	American National Standards Institute
BIAS	Biometric Identity Assurance Services
BioAPI	Biometric Application Programming Interface
BKA	Bundeskriminalamt (Federal Criminal Police Office of Germany)
BSP	Biometric Service Provider
BSC	Biometric Support Center
CAFIS	Cogent Automated Fingerprint Identification System
CAR	Criminal Ten-Print Submission (Answer Required)
CBEFF	Common Biometric Exchange Formats Framework
CJIS	Criminal Justice Information Services
CTISS	Common Terrorism Information Sharing Standards
DHS	Department of Homeland Security
DOD	Department of Defense
DOJ	Department of Justice
DOS	Department of State
EBTS	Electronic Biometric Transmission Specification
EFTS	Electronic Fingerprint Transmission Specification
FBI	Federal Bureau of Investigation
FCD	Final Committee Draft
FDIS	Final Draft International Standard
FIPS	Federal Information Processing Standard
GJXDM	Global Justice XML Data Model
HSPD	Homeland Security Presidential Directive
IAFIS	Integrated Automatic Fingerprint Identification System
ICAO	International Civil Aviation Organization

IDENT	Automatic Biometric Identification System
IDSM	Interim Data Sharing Model
IEC	International Electrotechnical Commission
IEPD	Information Exchange Package Document
INCITS	InterNational Committee for Information Technology Standards
INT-I	Interpol Implementation of the ANSI/NIST ITL 1 2000 Standard
ISO	International Organization for Standardization
ITL	Information Technology Laboratory
IXM	IDENT Exchange Messages
JPEG	Joint Photographic Experts Group
JTC	Joint Technical Committee
MRTD	Machine-Readable Travel Document
NCTC	National Counterterrorism Center
NGI	Next Generation Identification
NGI	Next Generation Identification
NIEM	National Information Exchange Model
NIST	National Institute of Standards and Technology
NISTIR	NIST Interagency Report
NSPD	National Security Presidential Directive
NSTC	National Science and Technology Council
OASIS	Organization for the Advancement of Structured Information Standards
OJP	Office of Justice Program
PDAM	Preliminary Draft Amendment
PNG	Portable Network Graphics
RT	Registered Traveler
RTIC	Registered Traveler Interoperability Consortium
SAP	Subject Acquisition Profile
SCA	Standards and Conformity Assessment
SDO	Standards Development Organization
SLA	Service Level Agreements

SMT	Scars, Mark and Tattoos
SOAP	Simple Object Access Protocol
TSC	Terrorist Screening Center
TWIC	Transportation Workers Identification Credential
TWPDES	Terrorist Watchlist Person Data Exchange Standard
USG	United States Government
US-VISIT	United States Visitor and Immigrant Status Indicator Technology
WD	Working Draft
WG	Working Group
WSQ	Wavelet Scalar Quantization
XML	Extensible Markup Language
2D	Two-Dimensional

Appendix A: Biometric Transaction (Service) Comparison

Generic Transaction	EFTS	INT-I v4.22b and v.5	IXM Operation	Germany	DOD EBTS v1.2
Fingerprint Identification	CAR – Criminal 10-Print Submission Answer Required CNA – Criminal 10-Print Submission No Answer Necessary Remote: TPIS – 10-Print Fingerprint Image Searches TPFS – 10-Print Fingerprint Features Search TPRS – 10-Print Rap Sheet Search FANC – Federal Applicant (No Charge) FAUF – Federal Applicant User Fee NFAP – Non-Federal Advanced Payment NFUF – Non-Federal Applicant User Fee MAP – Miscellaneous Applicant Civil DEK – Known Deceased DEU – Unknown Deceased MPR – Missing Person AMN – Amnesia Victim	CPS – Criminal Print-to-Print Search NPS – Noncriminal Print-to-Print Search	• Identify • Retrieve Identity • Identify Sync	CPS	CAR** TPRS MAP** FANC** DPRS – DOD flat-print rap sheet search

Generic Transaction	EFTS	INT-I v4.22b and v.5	IXM Operation	Germany	DOD EBTS v1.2
Identification Search Response	SRE – Submission Results – Electronic SRT – Search Results 10-Print ERRT – 10-Print Transaction Error NAR – Notification of Action Response ERRL – Latent Transaction Error	SRE – Search Results ERR – Error Message		SRE (includes Hit/No-Hit response) ERR	SRE LSR ERRT ERRL SRT LRE
Latent Search	LFS – Latent Fingerprint Image(s) Submission Remote: LFIS – Latent Fingerprint Image(s) Search LFFS – Latent Fingerprint Features Search LPNQ – Latent Penetration Query	MPS – Latent-to-Print Search PMS – Print-to-Latent Search MMS – Latent-to-Latent Search		MPS PMS MMS	LFIS LFFS
Latent Response	LSR – Latent Submission Results LPNR – Latent Penetration Query Response LSIR – Latent Search IDENT Response SRL – Search Results – Latent ULM – Unsolved Latent Match Response				
1:1 Verification			• Verify • Verify Sync		
Photo (FR) Search		CPP – Criminal Photo-to-Photo Search NPP – Noncriminal Photo-to-Photo Search			

Generic Transaction	EFTS	INT-I v4.22b and v.5	IXM Operation	Germany	DOD EBTS v1.2
Delete	DEK – Known Deceased DEU – Unknown Deceased ULD – Unsolved Latent Record Delete Request CPD – Subject Photo Delete Request	DFP – Delete from Print Collection USR – Remove Latent from Unidentified Latent Collection DPC – Delete From Photo Collection	• Delete Encounters		DEK** DEU**
Add*	ULAC – Unsolved Latent Add Confirm Request	ATP – Add to Print Collection USA – Add Latent to Unidentified Latent Collection APC – Add to Print Collection (incl. Photo)	• Add Biometrics • Add Disposition • Add Derogatory Information		
Update*	FIS – Fingerprint Image Submission	SUP – Substitute Prints into Existing 10-Print UPR – Update Request	• Deactivate Derogatory Information		
Queries (Retrievals)	IRQ – Image Request CPR Subject Photo Request	IRQ – Image Request DBS – Database Search CPR – Criminal Subject Photo Request	• Retrieve Criminal History • Preverify		IRQ VER – Verification Electronic Submission CPR
Notifications (back)	UULD – Unsolicited Unsolved Latent Delete		• Derogatory Update • Encounter • Enumerator • Enumerator Reassign		
Admin/Stats/Other	LRSQ – Latent Repository Statistics Query LSMQ – Latent Search Status & Modification Query	DIP – Disregard Individual Print Update			

Generic Transaction	EFTS	INT-I v4.22b and v.5	IXM Operation	Germany	DOD EBTS v1.2
Other Results	ULA – Unsolved Latent Add Confirm Response ULDR – Unsolved Latent Delete Response IRR – Image Request Response ISR – Image Summary Response ERRI – Image Transaction Error FISR – Fingerprint Image Submission Response PRR – Criminal Photo Request Response PDR – Photo Delete Response LRSR – Latent Repository Statistics Response LSMR – Latent Search Status & Modification Response ERRA – Administrative Transaction Error	IMR - Image Response PHR - Photo Response			IRR ISR ERRI PRR VRSP – Verification response-electronic (IDENT/non-IDENT info) EVER – verification error response

*Searches may also result in an add or update (and sometimes a delete).

**These DOD transactions have additional fields for DOD options (e.g., to include 2 iris, 1,000 ppi fingerprint images, and additional mug shots).

Appendix B: Cross Reference by Type-2 User-Defined Field Numbers and IXM Elements

Field Number	FBI EFTS and EBTS	DOD EBTS version 2.0	INT-I v4.22b and v5.0	Germany Implementing Agreement Proposal	IXM Element Mapping
2.001	LEN (Length)	LEN	LEN	LEN	
2.002	IDC (Image Designation Character)	IDC	IDC	IDC	
2.003	FFN (FBI File #)	FFN	SYS (System Info) (Version of INT-I spec)	SYS	
2.004	QDD (Query depth of detail-latent)		DAR (Date of Record)		
2.005	RET (Retention code)		DLU (Date of Last Update)		
2.006	ATN (Attention indicator-respond to)		SCT (Send Copy To)		
2.007	SCO (Send Copy To)	SCO	CNO (Case Number) (2-char country code plus latent case #)	CNO (2char Country Code/Case number)	
2.008			SQN (Sequence Number-latent)	SQN	
2.009	OCA (Originating Agency Case #)	OCA	MID (Latent Identifier)	MID	ActivityID
2.010	CIN (Contributor Case ID #-latent)	CIN (2 sub-fields)	CRN (Criminal Reference #) (begins with 2 char country code)	CRN (2 char country code/criminal reference #)	
2.011	CSX (Contributor Case ID Ext- latent)	CIX	ORN (Other Ref #)		

Field Number	FBI EFTS and EBTS	DOD EBTS version 2.0	INT-I v4.22b and v5.0	Germany Implementing Agreement Proposal	IXM Element Mapping
2.012	LCN (FBI Latent Case #)	LCN	MN1 (Misc ID #)	MN1 (CRN [2.010] for CPS or PMS transaction without country code)	
2.013	LCX (Latent case # extension)		MN2 (Misc ID #)	MN2 (contains CNO [2- 007] for MPS or MMS transaction without country code)	
2.014	FBI (FBI number)	FBI	MN3 (Misc ID #)	MN3 (SQN for MPS or MMS transaction)	PersonAssignedIDDetails PersonID ID IDTypecodeText "FBI"
2.015	SID (State ID #)	SID	MN4 (Misc ID #)	MN4 (MID for MPS or MMS transaction)	PersonAssignedIDDetails PersonID ID IDTypecodeText "SID"
2.016	SOC (Social Security Number)		MN5 (Misc ID #)		PersonAssignedIDDetails PersonID ID IDTypecodeText "SOC"
2.017	MNU (Misc. ID #)		FNU (Finger #/position)		PersonAssignedIDDetails PersonID ID [IAFIS Misc ID Number]
2.018	NAM (Name)		FIB (Fingerprint ID Byte/reason printed)		PersonName PersonGivenName PersonMiddlename PersonSurName

Field Number	FBI EFTS and EBTS	DOD EBTS version 2.0	INT-I v4.22b and v5.0	Germany Implementing Agreement Proposal	IXM Element Mapping
2.019	AKA (Aliases)		DPR (Date printed)		
2.020	POB		TOF (Time of fingerprinting)		PersonBirthPlaceCode
2.021	CTZ (Country of Citizenship-NCIC 2 char country code)		RFP (Reason fingerprinted- freetext)		PersonSocialDetails PersonCitizenshipCode Iso3166Alpha3
2.022	DOB		POA (Place of Arrest)		PersonBirthDate
2.023	AGR (Age range)		OBU (Owning Bureau)		
2.024	SEX	SEX	DON (Date of Notice)		PersonPhysicalDetails PersonSexCode
2.025	RAC (Race)		SIM (Station Inputting latent)		PersonPhysicalDetails PersonRaceCode
2.026	SMT (Scars- Marks- & Tattoos)		QLM (Quality Measure)		
2.027	HGT (Height)		CCP (Coarse Classif. of Patterns)		PersonPhysicalDetails PersonHeightMeasure
2.028	HTR (Height range)		FCP (Fine Classif. of Patterns)		
2.029	WGT (Weight)		NLF (Nominal File / msg formatting)		PersonPhysicalDetails PersonWeightMeasure
2.030	WTR (Weight range)		NAM (Name)		
2.031	EYE (Eye color)		MNA (Maiden Name)		PersonPhysicalDetails PersonEyeColorCode
2.032	HAI (Hair color)	HAI	ADD (Address)		PersonPhysicalDetails PersonHairColorCode
2.033	FPC (NCIC Fingerprint Classif- rtn- latent)		TRU (True Identity- how determined)		

CI:
March 8, 2010

Field Number	FBI EFTS and EBTS	DOD EBTS version 2.0	INT-I v4.22b and v5.0	Germany Implementing Agreement Proposal	IXM Element Mapping
2.034	PAT (Pattern Level Classification)		AKA (Aliases)		
2.035	PPA (Palmprints available indicator)		DOB (Date of Birth)		
2.036	PHT (Photo available indicator)		DBR (DOB range)		
2.037	RFP (Reason fingerprinted)	RFP	POB (Place of Birth) ISO 3166 Alpha2		AcitivityReasonText
2.038	DPR (Date fingerprinted)		NAT (Nationality) ISO 3166 Alpha2		PersonBiometricDetails PersonFingerprintSet BiometricCaptureDate
2.039	EAD (Employer & address)		SEX		
2.040	OCP (Occupation)		COL (Skin Color of Subject)		
2.041	RES (Residence- subject address)		HGT (Height)		
2.042	MIL (Military Code- submitter)		BLD (Build)		
2.043	TSR (Type of search requested)		HAI (Hair color/style)		
2.044	GEO (Geographic area of search)	GEO	FAC (Face description)		
2.045	DOA (Date of Arrest)	DOA	LAN (Languages spoken)		
2.046	DOS (DOA suffix)		PHO (Photo #)		
2.047	ASL (Arrest segment literal)	ASL	PSP (Passport #)		
2.048	CSR (Civil Search Requested indicator)		MAR (Marks)		

Field Number	FBI EFTS and EBTS	DOD EBTS version 2.0	INT-I v4.22b and v5.0	Germany Implementing Agreement Proposal	IXM Element Mapping
2.049	EID (Employee Identification #-*EBTS*)		OCC (Occupation)		
2.050			WNG (Warning-dangerous subject)		
2.051	CSL (Court segment literal)	CSL	MDO (Modus Operandi)		
2.052			GAC (Geographical Area of Crime)		
2.053	OFC (Offense category)	OFC	GSA (Geographical Area of Search)		
2.054	SSD (Custody or supervisory status start date)	SSD	OTY (Offense Type)		
2.055	SLE (Custody or supervisory status literal)	SLE	DOO (Date of Offense)		
2.056	ICO (Identification comments- caution)	ICO	DOR (DOO range)		
2.057	FNR (Finger numbers requested)		DSR (DOO search range)		
2.058			TOO (Time of Offense)		
2.059	SRF (Search Results Findings)	SRF	TOR (TOO range)		
2.060	MSG (Status/Error Message)	MSG	TSR (TOO search range)		
2.061	CST (Case Title- latent)	CST	TLM (Time Limit- for processing)		
2.062	IMT (Image Type)		ICP (Flag – Interpol Secr. Forwarding)		

Field Number	FBI EFTS and EBTS	DOD EBTS version 2.0	INT-I v4.22b and v5.0	Germany Implementing Agreement Proposal	IXM Element Mapping
2.063	PTD (Person type designator)	PTD	INF (Additional info)	INF(Additional Information) (If included in SRE for PMS – indicates the finger that caused a hit – otherwise optional)	
2.064	CAN (Candidate List)	CAN	RLS (Respondents list / candidates)	RLS (type of transaction plus "I" for Hit or "N" for no hit; sequence ID for candidate results and total # candidates)	
2.065	RSR (Repository Statistic Response)	RSR	COU (Recipient countries' databases searched)		
2.066			RES (Result – Address responses to be sent)		
2.067	IMA (Image Capture Equipment)		ALF (Alert Flag – latents)		
2.068			TCF (Target Criminal Flag – always search)		
2.069	ETC (Estimated time to complete search)	ETC	IDF (Identified Flag – multiple latents)		
2.070	RAP (Rap sheet requested)	RAP	MPF (Latent Priority Flag)		
2.071	ACN (Action to be taken)	CAN	TUF (Tie up flag – latent linkages)		
2.072	FIU (Fingerprint image updated)		RNK (Rank of signing officer)		
2.073	CRI (Controlling agency ID)	CRI	DSG (Date of signature)		ORIID (Organization ID)

Field Number	FBI EFTS and EBTS	DOD EBTS version 2.0	INT-I v4.22b and v5.0	Germany Implementing Agreement Proposal	IXM Element Mapping
2.074	FGP (Finger Position)		ERM (Status/Error Message)	ERM	
2.075	ERS (Electronic rapsheet)	ERS	FFN (Father's Family Name) v5		
2.076	PRI (Priority- latent search)	PRI	MMN (Mother's Maiden Name) v5		
2.077	CFS (Cancel Fingerprint Search)	CFS			
2.078	PEN (Penetration Query response)				
2.079	NCR (Number of Candidate Images returned)	NCR			
2.080	EXP (Response explanation)	EXP	BRT (Broadcast Request To)		
2.081	UCN (Universal control #)				
2.082	REC (Response code – photo transaction)	REC			
2.083	ULF (flag – add to unsolved latent file)		FPR (Finger Present – missing)		

Biometric Standards Requirements for US-VISIT

Field Number	FBI EFTS and EBTS	DOD EBTS version 2.0	INT-I v4.22b and v5.0	Germany Implementing Agreement Proposal	IXM Element Mapping
2.084	AMP (Amputated or bandaged – missing)	AMP			PersonBiometricDetails PersonFingerprintSet Fingerprint FingerprintPatternCode [Single Rolled Print] *IXM also lists following for 2.084* PersonBiometricDetails PersonFingerprintSet Fingerprint FingerprintFingerSegment FingerprintPatternCode [Identification Flat Segment]
2.085	CRN (Civil Record #)	CRN	ARI (Additional Response Info)		
2.086	SCNA (AFIS segment ctrl #- transaction #)	SCNA			
2.087	TAA (Treat as Adult)	TAA			
2.088	NOT (Note field- latent)	NOT			
2.089	MSC (Match Score)	MSC			
2.091	RCD1 (Ridge Core Delta 1 for subpattern class)				
2.092	RCD2 (Ridge Core Delta 2 for subpattern class)				
2.093	SPCN SPECIAL POPULATION COGNIZANT FILE NUMBER				

Field Number	FBI EFTS and EBTS	DOD EBTS version 2.0	INT-I v4.22b and v5.0	Germany Implementing Agreement Proposal	IXM Element Mapping
2.094	CCN (FBI court case number)	CCN			
2.095	RFR REQUEST FEATURES RECORD				
2.096	RPR REQUEST PHOTO RECORD	RPR			
2.098	NDR NAME OF DESIGNATED REPOSITORY				
2.099	SAN STATE ARREST NUMBER				
2.2001	NAM1 NAME-ONE				
2.2002	NAM2 NAME-TWO				
2.2003	NAM3 NAME-THREE				
2.2004	NAM4 NAME-FOUR				
2.2005	NAM5 NAME-FIVE				
2.2006	CSF CASCADED SEARCH FLAG				
2.2007	SDOB SUBMITTED DATE OF BIRTH				
2.2008	SNAM SUBMITTED NAME				
2.2009	PTY PHOTO TYPE				
2.2010	NIR No. of Images Requested				
2.2011	*tbd RAP BACK Verification Status				
2.012	IIR IRIS IMAGES REQUESTED				

Field Number	FBI EFTS and EBTS	DOD EBTS version 2.0	INT-I v4.22b and v5.0	Germany Implementing Agreement Proposal	IXM Element Mapping
2.013	DMI DISPOSITION MAINTENANCE INDICATOR				
2.2014	*tbd RAP BACK ELIGIBILITY				
2.2015	*tbd RAP BACK EXPIRATION DATE				
2.2016	DNAF DNA FLAG				
2.2017	DORI DNA LOCATION				
2.2018	DNAC DNA IN CODIS FLAG				
2.2019	SEAL SEAL ARREST FLAG				
2.2020	*tbd RAP BACK RECIPIENT				
2.2021	IFS IDENTIFICATION FIREARMS				
2.301		BLO (Location-v1.2 only- not in v2.0			
2.303		DOD_NO DOD Number			
2.306		GEO_CORD Geographic Coordinate (v2.0)			
2.307		DATUM_ID Geographic Coordinate			
2.310		PER_TYPE (biometric subject personnel type)			
2.316		RMS (request mug shot)			
2.317		RIS (request secondary search)			

Field Number	FBI EFTS and EBTS	DOD EBTS version 2.0	INT-I v4.22b and v5.0	Germany Implementing Agreement Proposal	IXM Element Mapping
2.318		XML (XML-based rap sheet)			
2.320				ENC (Expected Number of Candidates)	
2.321		CORD_OTHER			
2.322		CORD_UTM			
2.350		ALERT		RTD (Reference to Database- *where hits were found*)	
2.351		ARSP			
2.352		LOOKUP			
2.353		SN			
2.8000		NAME			
2.8001		SUBJ_ADDR			
2.8002		SUBJ_CNTCT			
2.8003		DOB Subject Birth Date			
2.8004		POB Subject birth place			
2.8005		DOD subject death date			
2.8006		POD Subject death place			
2.8007		CTZ subject citizenship			
2.8008		Biometric subject Ethnic/racial characteristic			
2.8009		HGT Subject height			
2.8010		WGT			
2.8011		LEYE			

Biometric Standards Requirements for US-VISIT

Field Number	FBI EFTS and EBTS	DOD EBTS version 2.0	INT-I v4.22b and v5.0	Germany Implementing Agreement Proposal	IXM Element Mapping
2.8012		REYE			
2.8013		BLOOD			
2.8014		VITAL			
2.8015		OTHER_PHYS			
2.8016		MAR_STAT			
2.8017		IASSOC			
2.8018		GRPMBR			
2.8019		COL_IDENT Collected identification			
2.8020		COL_APP_ASGN_IDENT			
2.8021		CLEAR Subject clearance			
2.8022		COMPART			
2.8023		SUBJ_COM Subject comment			
2.8024		SUBJ_COM subject US person indicator			
2.8025		SUBJ_COM subject derogatory comment			
2.8100		BLO Collection location			
2.8101		COLL_DATE			
2.8102		ENCTR_MSN			
2.8103		COL_RSN			
2.8104		OPER			
2.8105		CONVEY			
2.8106		EVENT